Turning to Earth

TURNING TO EARTH

Stories of
Ecological Conversion

F. Marina Schauffler

For Ann. With all good wishes in your turning, Marina Schauffler October 2003

University of Virginia Press

Charlottesville & London

University of Virginia Press
© 2003 by F. Marina Schauffler
All rights reserved
Printed in the United States of America
on acid-free paper
First published 2003

1 3 5 7 9 8 6 4 2

Library of Congress Cataloging-in-Publication Data

Schauffler, F. Marina.
   Turning to Earth : stories of ecological conversion / F. Marina
Schauffler.
      p. cm.
Includes bibliographical references (p.   ) and index.
   ISBN 0-8139-2186-4 (acid-free paper) — ISBN 0-8139-2187-2
(pbk. : acid-free paper)
      1. American fiction—20th century—History and criticism.
2. Nature in literature. 3. Environmental protection—Moral
and ethical aspects. 4. Natural history—United States—Histo-
riography. 5. Conservation of natural resources in literature.
6. Environmental protection in literature. 7. Philosophy of
nature in literature. 8. Conversion in literature. 9. Ecology in
literature. 10. Ecocriticism. I. Title.
   PS374 .N3 S33 2003
   823'.5409355—dc21

                                                    2002154233

*For the Island
and the Family It Joins*

Contents

Turning to Earth

Introduction

Seeking the Whole at the Center

Each fall, my home state of Maine holds a coastwide cleanup day in which several thousand volunteers collect accumulated debris from beaches, rocky shores, and salt marshes. During several years in which I helped organize this garbage-picking marathon, we managed to recruit successively more volunteers, gather more waste, and draw more media coverage. Consequently the event was deemed a success. Yet a month or two after the cleanup, the debris would be back. Despite federal legislation that bans ocean dumping of plastics, the oil containers and soda bottles kept appearing. Clearly we could gather garbage indefinitely without ever stemming the tide.

To help prevent pollution at the source, cleanup organizers began distributing educational posters and running public service ads. Yet still the debris washed in. Information alone could not solve the problem: people were not tossing debris into the ocean because they did not know that plastics could endure for centuries. They were dumping trash overboard because they saw the sea as a vast wilderness that would absorb it. And they believed the items were—as marketers claimed—"disposable."

Only by transforming entrenched beliefs like these, I came to see, could we achieve lasting environmental change. Too often we rely on "Earth-saving tips" that mitigate the symptoms of degradation without addressing root causes. I had adopted many of these pointers myself and counseled others to do the same, but now this simplistic approach seemed painfully inadequate. The magnitude and severity of ecological problems demand far more substantive changes in how we live. Instead of advising people to reduce their use of lawn chemicals and to keep their cars well tuned, I wanted to suggest that they rethink grass monocultures altogether and that they bicycle instead of driving.

Yet it was hard enough to get people to adopt the easy tips, the minor modifications that did not disrupt their comfortable but damaging modes of life. More substantive environmental reform clearly would require a widespread change of heart. What could touch people deeply enough to inspire such a transformation?

Part of the answer, I sensed, lay in confronting the ecological paradox with which we live: we want to dwell in healthy, natural settings, yet we routinely make choices (regarding consumption, recreation, diet, and transportation) that degrade local and global ecosystems. We tend to view environmental crises as occurring outside us, rather than admitting that they stem from who we are and how we live. Consequently, we seek to cure complex problems like global warming and habitat destruction with technological, political, or economic "quick fixes" that won't require any change in our accustomed ways of life.

This dilemma reflects a long-standing cultural divide that has cleaved Western thought and human identity since the Enlightenment. Most of our historical, literary, and religious texts view humans as distinct from the natural world, living in a "civilized" realm inherently at odds with the "wild." The schism reveals itself in how we speak about the larger ecological whole: the terms *environment* and *nature* connote a realm apart from humanity and culture rather than a whole in which we are intimately embedded. Emphasis on sound "environmental management" assumes that humans oversee other species instead of participating with them in an interdependent community.

Compounding this ecological schizophrenia are philosophical and religious traditions that view humans as the crowning glory of evolution. Anthropocentric belief systems place humans above nature, which comes to be seen as the repository of all other life-forms. Our privileged status presumably entitles us to use other beings and the elemental Earth as "resources" without concern for their intrinsic needs. Anthropocentrism contributes to environmental exploitation and degradation by sanctioning wasteful and polluting modes of production and consumption (such as factory farming, pesticide spraying, and clear-cutting); it also leads to physical ailments and mental dis-ease within the human community.

Even ardent environmentalists who acknowledge life's essential interdependence can get caught in these entrenched belief systems. They argue at times that nature should take precedence over human needs, failing to see that upending the traditional hierarchy provides no lasting resolution. Preservationists inadvertently perpetuate this cultural chasm in their quest to secure pristine wilderness areas "untainted" by any human presence. Rather than healing the enduring divide, they merely reverse the timeworn roles by sanctifying the wild and vilifying the human.

To heal this schism and forge a new relation to the natural whole, we must begin to look inward—reassessing who we are and how we behave. The transformation requires more than a reform of old habits: it calls for a change that is radical in the original sense (*radix*, in Latin, meaning root). Radical measures seek to address the heart of environmental problems, changing the assumptions that fuel destructive habits. Such a substantive change will take us beyond our reliance on cognitive information, regulations, and economic incentives—means that have fostered significant environmental reforms but have failed to prompt an enduring change in our actions and attitudes.

Changing from the Inside Out

Restoring the health of *outer ecology*—the collective web of life and elemental matter in which we participate—depends on a renewal of *inner ecology*, the spiritual beliefs and ethical values that guide our actions. Inner and outer ecology complement each other, forming an indivisible whole. Ecology originally meant "household," or "home," deriving from the Greek word *oikos*. In this ancient sense, ecology

involves learning how to be at home on Earth. Rather than reinforcing the abiding cultural schism between humans and nature, the
distinction between inner and outer ecology may help to reconcile
modes of understanding that have been separated for too long. It
allows us to perceive the natural world in ways that are spiritual and
moral as well as scientific and political.

Nearly every facet of the environmental field—from the acad-
emy to the legislature—currently neglects the critical role of inner
ecology. Environmental activists, fearing ridicule by opponents, avoid
mention of spiritual or emotional bonds to other species that might
earn them the epithet "tree-hugger." Environmental research and
teaching concentrate on science and policy, overlooking how philosophy, religion, and psychology shape environmental values and
practices. Politicians scrupulously avoid discussion of inner change,
even as they acknowledge the limits of legislative solutions.

This consistent neglect of inner ecology may stem from our cultural attachment to scientific materialism, an intellectual tradition
that reveres the factual and quantitative and devalues dimensions of
life that cannot be weighed, measured, or charted. Many individuals have such strong faith in the truth of science and the deliverance
of technology that they no longer see a need for the spiritual beliefs
and ethical values that shape inner ecology. Environmental reform,
in their view, becomes solely a matter of crafting new rules and regulations based on the best available data.

The director of an environmental group once asked me, in a job
interview, where I stood on the spectrum that runs from "hard-
edged advocacy" to contemplative means of honoring Earth. It was
clear which end of the spectrum he valued, but I couldn't give him
the answer he sought. Each of us, I replied, needs to span that spectrum—engaging in environmental planning, lobbying, and policy
making (to help sustain outer ecology) while simultaneously striving to renew our spiritual and moral bonds with the natural world
(thereby restoring inner ecology). If we neglect the inner dimensions—as many individuals and organizations in the environmental
movement do—then we risk working against pollution and degra-

dation without knowing what it is we are working for. Inner ecology provides an essential complement so that we are not simply turning *from* the destructive forces and habits of Western culture. We are turning *toward* a new vision of humans' place within the whole.

In recent years, scholars and activists have begun to explore facets of this neglected inner realm. The emerging field of ecopsychology is describing ways in which our individual psyches are intimately bound to the elemental Earth. Ecocritics are reassessing literary texts, seeing what they tell us about our place within the natural world. Scholars in environmental ethics are exploring how moral principles and patterns of thought shape our relations to other species.

Religious and spiritual seekers are turning their attention to Earth-centered belief systems that view the living world as sacred. Within Western culture, these beliefs take shape in a wide range of private and unstructured forms, as well as in communal traditions like those of Native Americans. Earth-centered faiths encompass an interdependent worldview that challenges the culture's prevailing anthropocentrism and strives to honor all beings, forging a harmonious relation with the whole through worship and ethical conduct. Earth-based believers represent only a small fraction of the general population, but their perspectives have gained credence as more people come to acknowledge the depth and breadth of ecological ills.

Among environmental activists and philosophers, proponents of "deep ecology" have focused most attention on the inner ecological realm, describing sources of our estrangement from the natural whole. This eclectic and diverse movement holds that the elemental world has intrinsic value (apart from its utility for humans) and that humans should draw upon its rich biological diversity only to meet vital needs. Deep ecologists fuse abstract philosophy with grassroots advocacy, calling for dramatic societal change and modes of living that place fewer demands on the Earth. Yet even their treatises rarely suggest how to effect an ecological awakening within ourselves and others.

Surprisingly few of the new texts that explore philosophical, spiritual, and psychological dimensions of inner ecology address the dynamics of change. Finding little guidance among these scholarly works, I began to reflect on my own lived experience. My impulse to heal the Earth clearly comes from a passionate bond to place, an active immersion in the mystery and complexity of being. That engagement with the natural world fuels my ecological commitment, making actions on behalf of Earth expressions of spiritual gratitude more than of ethical duty. Having read many autobiographical accounts of individuals' bonds with the natural whole, I knew that my experience was not unusual. By drawing together personal stories of ecological awakening, I hoped to uncover dynamics of inner ecology that might help to renew the outer world.

Ecological Conversion: The Dynamics of Change

In this book, I outline the catalysts and characteristics of *ecological conversion*, an encompassing transformation that touches every facet of an individual's life—physical, spiritual, emotional, psychological, and political. The term connotes a religious transformation (*re-ligare*, in Latin, meaning "to bind together"): through conversion, an individual reconnects with the ecological whole, re-visioning her place in the world and reforming her life accordingly. Scholar Steven Rockefeller observes that religious change depends not on intellect but on will, "the staking of the whole being" on a particular vision.[1] When an individual stakes her being on a vision of ecological wholeness and connection, the contours of both inner and outer ecology can change.

Viewing environmental reform in terms of conversion extends the parameters of contemporary environmental discussion. It highlights the spiritual and moral dimensions of change and the need for a wholehearted reassessment of how we live. A better understanding of inner ecology could help move us beyond a blinkered focus on policies, regulations, and technical innovations as the sole means to substantive change. We might begin to take more personal responsibility for the world we have created and to seek new ways to cherish and sustain the living Earth.

This exploratory work ventures into terrain not yet charted by traditional disciplines. Even the newer fields of ecocriticism, environmental philosophy, and ecopsychology have focused little on these inner dynamics, in part because conversion stubbornly resists empirical study. Quantitative research rarely illuminates this subjective and variable process, and even qualitative methods fail to capture its complexity. Conversion eludes facile descriptions, having no definitive list of prerequisites or outcomes. It represents "an experience to be lived and tasted, rather than theorized about."[2]

Most of us *have* lived and tasted conversion, in one form or other, because it is human nature to change in response to experience. We may not view ourselves as converts to new political ideologies, economic worldviews, or health practices, but we recognize that our lives are governed by different perspectives and priorities than they once were.

In the case of ecological converts, life experiences move them toward a greater appreciation and concern for the natural whole. Living in a culture deeply estranged from other species and the elemental world, converts to Earth struggle to achieve—for themselves and others—a fundamental sense of belonging. Their ecological commitment grows through an active process of "turning," in which they relinquish societal truths and forge new beliefs and practices. By striving to realize positive ideals, they move beyond the customary trap of environmental activism: continually reacting against destructive trends.

The turn to Earth is rarely a straight trajectory from old life to new; more commonly it involves a cycling back, a re-turning. Returning creates a spiral of growth where old patterns and perspectives are continually incorporated into the new. Cycling back to past experiences does not constitute backsliding or regression but an essential step in a spiral evolution.

The process of turning to Earth is both more circuitous and more gradual than we might expect, having come to associate conversion with revival-meeting accounts of sudden and dramatic transformations. Among traditional religious converts, the abrupt turn—epitomized by Saul on the road to Damascus—appears to be a common means of spiritual awakening. Yet the writings of ecological converts reveal few such marked transformations; more often, individuals undergo a slow, progressive form of conversion. Their gradual turns, although less dramatic than the stereotype, are no less active. Some evidence even suggests that more subtle and protracted conversions have more lasting effects than do abrupt turns, in which surficial qualities may change without altering the deeper self.[3]

Incremental turns can take varied forms. Some involve a steady accumulation of insights where the convert, gaining strength in his convictions, begins to live with a stronger sense of life purpose and vision. In this form of conversion, the direction of growth often is set early in life. Reintegrating abandoned or neglected parts of the self can help the convert to become more whole. This process may occur, for example, when someone returns to live where she was raised—reconnecting with a place that once was part of her. Or it may happen through the act of writing, re-collecting neglected dimensions of one's past.

Another form of conversion, paradoxically, requires people to gradually shed their accumulated masks and habits. Converts characterize this process not as gaining a new identity or integrating parts of their lives but as a gradual excavation down to an essential center—a foundational sense of belonging to the whole. Poet Linda Hogan asserts that "growth comes from removing and removing, ceasing, undoing, and letting ourselves drop down or even fall into the core of our living being."[4] What lies at the center is not so much a static set of values or ecological commandments but a mode of connection, a spiritual kinship that shapes our relation to the world.

The process of inner excavation may lead a convert to forfeit beliefs and practices that do not align with core values. These acts of relinquishment can hold overtones of repentance, reminiscent of more conventional forms of conversion. Repentance implies a recognition of past sins and a resolve to live differently. Although this dimension is less pronounced in ecological conversion, the turning does represent a simultaneous movement *from* past ways and *toward* a new vision.

Certain experiences—some of them consciously planned, others wholly unanticipated—seem to predispose individuals to awakening. Ecological converts seek out opportunities for spiritual communion with the natural whole: they are, in writer Edward Abbey's words, "prospectors for revelation."[5] Yet their quests are not always rewarded. Conversion, they learn, cannot be choreographed. The process happens through a fortuitous mix of choice and chance, when "will and grace are joined."[6]

The aspect of chance or grace may be harder to discern than the aspect of choice or will. Converts to conventional faiths commonly portray their experience as a forceful calling in which God directs them down paths they never would have chosen. Those who turn to Earth rarely cite the hand of God in this way, and typically they stand outside institutional and creedal faith traditions. Yet they acknowledge that their lives are governed by a strong sense of the sacred, an abiding wonder and gratitude in the mystery of being. Spirituality, in their view, constitutes "living in accordance with the dynamism of life."[7] Since the conviction of a sacred essence within the world resists formulation into creeds and may be experienced most profoundly outside institutional structures, the term *spiritual*—rather than *religious*—best describes the process by which ecological converts affirm their covenantal bonds with the whole. Their spirituality, while rarely marked by traditional religious rites, becomes an ongoing creative act that infuses every facet of their lives.

The spiritual conviction that marks ecological conversion seldom extends to the zealous evangelism that can characterize more traditional religious conversions. Turning to Earth does not lead to dogmatic belief or fundamentalist fervor, in which converts adhere to a rigid ethic or devote their lives to the quasi-institution of environmentalism. Their faith in Earth is grounded in lived experience rather than in religious or political doctrine.

Ecological Practice: A Living Expression of Change

By definition, conversion implies "a change in the self sufficiently deep and lasting to bring about a change of conduct and bearing in the world."[8] The ecological convert is called to revise foundational beliefs *and* to consciously embody new values. The ongoing effort to live with ecological integrity can be seen as a disciplined practice. It is not the culmination of conversion so much as the form that supports it.

Like other modes of spiritual practice, an ecological practice engages the whole being. It touches every facet of life from the intellectual and emotional to the physical. In this respect, an ecological practice differs from what are commonly termed "environmental practices"—mundane habits and household actions intended to benefit the natural world. Environmental practices such as recycling or conserving energy may be small manifestations of a larger ecological practice, a holistic commitment to live in ways that honor one's bonds with the Earth.

Although termed a singular practice, the lived expression of ecological connections can take diverse forms that reflect the unique circumstances and disposition of the convert. These forms may be harder to discern than with converts to conventional faiths where dogma and tradition dictate the contours of practice. Ecological converts express their core beliefs through markedly different types of practice. A concern with the welfare of other beings, for example, could take the form of vegetarianism in one person, while another might subsistence hunt with bow and arrow (pursuing prey in a manner that seeks to honor the spirit and life of the animal). What unites the different forms is an ongoing commitment to acknowledge and deepen connections with the ecological whole.

Outward evidence of these bonds may be slow to manifest, since the turn to Earth is often a gradual, cyclical process. When an individual begins to experience a deep sense of connection with animals, for example, she might at first commune silently with other beings, learn more about native flora and fauna, or quietly mourn the loss of a neighborhood tree. As the conversion proceeds and a sense of reciprocity grows, the convert might make more obvious changes—such as conserving wildlife habitat or advocating on behalf of threatened species. The form of an ecological practice evolves in response to both outer circumstances and inner imperatives.

Because turns to Earth are gradual, the narrative evidence of change can be subtle, with threads scattered through numerous works. Diffuse signs of inner transformation have made it hard for scholars and critics to identify ecological conversion as a distinct phenomenon. In this work, I attempt to draw together those scattered threads, weaving them into a whole that reveals essential patterns in this elusive process.

Stories of Conversion: Windows into the Heart of Change

To understand the subtle dynamics of ecological conversion, we depend on the stories of those who have turned to Earth. Their accounts describe the terrain of inner ecology and suggest ways to strengthen our connections with the natural whole. Narratives play a powerful role in shaping spiritual understanding and moral action: they can lead us closer to truth than facts can, offering a depth of meaning—a resonance with the real—not found in cognitive schemes or abstract theories. We often depend on stories to inspire new actions and attitudes.

This work draws on the stories of writers who have experienced ecological conversion. Their capacity for introspection and their facility with words make them ideal candidates to portray the internal dynamics that propel substantive change. Writers also document their experiences over time, an essential element in assessing turns to Earth that unfold over years and decades.

Informal accounts of ecological conversion appear in many autobiographical works of "nature writing" (nonfiction that describes encounters with the natural world). Because nature writers have traditionally focused primarily on the external environment, those who describe the dynamic interplay between inner and outer ecology are more accurately termed *ecological writers,* which suggests an integration of human and natural realms that helps dissolve the traditional divide between them. The writers included in this book understand ecology in a philosophical and practical sense that reflects the term's earliest meaning of "household," or "home." Ecological writers share an abiding desire to be at home on Earth and express that deep sense of belonging through words.

In their explorations of outer and inner domains, ecological writers benefit from a rich legacy that extends back centuries through transcendentalism to British romanticism. Romantics like Blake, Coleridge, and the Wordsworths wrote with the fervor of religious testimony, honoring the intricate and infinite connections within nature. Railing against industrial mechanization and the Cartesian worldview, they strove to restore a vital natural community in which humans would live as conscious participants rather than mindless destroyers. That change, they believed, could be inspired by the natural world if humans opened themselves to its wisdom.

American transcendentalists built on the foundations of British romanticism and German idealism, exploring what they termed the "correspondence" between spirit and matter. Works by two of the movement's leading voices, Ralph Waldo Emerson and Henry David Thoreau, have left a deep imprint on generations of ecological writers. Both these visionaries strove to embody a new relation to the natural world, living with an acute appreciation for the complex web of being: "Our whole life," Thoreau wrote, "is startlingly moral. There is never an instant's truce between virtue and vice."[9] His writings document that ongoing struggle to challenge societal norms and forge a niche for himself within the greater natural whole.

Many contemporary ecological writers find that their experiences recapitulate those recorded by literary predecessors. Despite significant changes in the natural and cultural environment over the centuries, the dynamics of inner ecology seem to be similar. This parallel in experience suggests that ecological conversion is not a phenomenon confined to contemporary times.

Generations of ecological writers have shared accounts of their awakenings, fusing tales of inspiration with exhortations to change. While many resist overt proselytizing, they clearly seek to touch and transform the hearts and minds of their readers. They seem to maintain a core faith in human potential that persists alongside strong societal critiques. Ecological writing remains a "literature of hope" in its conviction that heightened consciousness can lead to substantive political change.[10] Those writers who turn to Earth and commit themselves to a sustained ecological practice hope that others may follow a similar path, coming to lead integrated lives "in which their experience and knowledge of the natural world are consistent with their social and political vision, their spiritual lives, and their aesthetic."[11]

The Convert's Word

The reflective personal accounts of ecological writers can best be seen as a form of natural autobiography, a memoir of their evolving relation to the more-than-human world. The process of tracing their life histories in this context helps individuals redefine their place within the whole.

In telling their stories, writers cannot help but re-create themselves. They invariably edit their experience, potentially distorting the historical record. Their stories represent a narrative rather than a historical truth. On this basis, some anthropologists have dismissed autobiography as "useful chiefly for the study of the perversion of truth by memory."[12] This remark reflects a positivist tradition in which the only valid truth is an empirical one. Spiritual transformation, though, resists conforming to this measure. Drawing on deep and profound levels of wisdom, conversion holds truths that defy cognitive explanation (as Pascal observed, "the heart has its reasons which reason knows nothing of").

The writers included in this work generally recognize that their truth is subjective and that their values are not universal norms. Nonetheless, they appear determined to live by certain principles. These writers characterize their lives in terms that counter post-modern tendencies to repudiate the concept of a self or to postulate the existence of many selves. They tend to view themselves as having, in one writer's words, a "bedrock self" that provides continuity in the midst of dynamic change.[13] They acknowledge that language shapes our world and our place within it, but they resist the impulse to deny that the world exists apart from our constructions. Since I seek to portray the truth of their experience, I rely primarily on the concepts and terminology that they employ.

In sifting through the life stories of ecological writers, I have tried to enter into their narratives, assuming the role of a literary participant-observer rather than that of a critical outsider. The subjective and spiritual nature of these accounts dictates an empathic approach. My concern is not with *how* they write but with *what* they claim to experience. Rather than analyzing the form and structure of their works, I have sought to examine their narratives through a religious lens, using spiritual concepts (such as conversion, practice, and revelation) to characterize the process and draw parallels between ecological and conventional forms of awakening.

My focus was split between a broad survey of numerous ecological writers and a more detailed examination of works by six individuals. This attempt to synthesize micro- and macro-levels grew from a desire to situate the primary subjects in a larger context, as part of a diverse community. By covering both levels simultaneously, I hope to offer readers a wide-angle view into the realm of inner ecology.

With such a small number of primary writers represented, a claim to portray "common elements" of their conversion experience may seem inflated. How could an "exploratory model" of *anything* be based on a sample size of just six individuals? Preliminary research into the lives of other ecological writers, though, appears to confirm the transformational patterns evident in this modest initial sample.

The primary six individuals became the focus of my research through a process that was both systematic and intuitive. Since the dynamics of inner ecology are invariably influenced by the milieu

in which an individual lives, I chose writers from one country—
the United States—during a clearly defined historical period (the
late twentieth century). All of these writers published their major
works after 1945. Consequently they shared in the cultural climate
of postwar America: the rapid technological development and material growth of the 1950s as well as the Cold War. They also felt the
influence of the environmental movement that emerged in the
1960s, part of a broad wave of youthful idealism and social rebellion.

Featured Ecological Writers

Within the small sample of writers included here, I sought a balance
of genders and an array of geographic loyalties, ethnic backgrounds,
and religious influences. Since there were any number of combina-
tions that would meet those criteria, I selected writers who—by my
subjective measure—seemed best able to describe the dynamics of
their inner transformations. To provide greater diversity, accounts
from dozens of other ecological converts supplement stories by the
following six writers.

EDWARD ABBEY (1927–1989) moved from the Appalachian foothills of western Pennsylvania to the Southwest during his twenties
and made his home there—writing and working temporary jobs for
supplemental income (including seventeen seasons as a fire lookout
and park ranger). Abbey held undergraduate and graduate degrees
in philosophy and wrote his master's thesis on anarchy. Rather than
pursuing a conventional academic career, he chose to live and write
on his own terms in the place he loved. Abbey considered himself
foremost a novelist, but he is best known for nonfiction essays that
reflect his irreverent humor, iconoclastic nature, and vehement concern for preserving the Southwest. The works that reveal most
about Abbey's turn to Earth are *Abbey's Road, Desert Solitaire, The
Journey Home,* and his published journal compilations (particularly
Confessions of a Barbarian).

RACHEL CARSON (1907–1964) obtained a master's degree in zoology before securing a job with the federal Bureau of Fisheries, where she worked her way up to become director of publications. Alongside her scientific expertise, Carson had a deep passion for the living world that emerged through her creative nonfiction. Outside work, she drafted essays about marine life that eventually took shape in three popular books. After leaving her government post, Carson turned her formidable energy to the research and writing of *Silent Spring*, during which she was diagnosed with malignant breast cancer. The final months of her life were spent testifying to the need for humans to act with greater humility and care in relation to the natural world. Carson's personal reflections on ecological conversion are most evident in *The Sense of Wonder, Always, Rachel* (collected letters), and *The House of Life*, a biography by her editor and friend Paul Brooks.

N. SCOTT MOMADAY (1934–) was raised in Arizona and New Mexico, spending extensive time at the Navajo reservation in Shiprock and the Jemez Pueblo. He received a Wallace Stegner Creative Writing Fellowship to attend Stanford University and later completed a doctorate in American literature. In an academic career that might have led him away from his strong connections to place and tribal traditions, Momaday has consciously maintained those ties. Alongside teaching, Momaday has written books of autobiographical prose, fiction, and poetry and has done paintings and drawings that fuse tribal and ancestral stories with personal and historical reflections. The works that best depict his turn to Earth are *The Man Made of Words, The Way to Rainy Mountain*, and a series of interviews by Charles Woodard entitled *Ancestral Voice*.

SCOTT RUSSELL SANDERS (1945–) spent his earliest years in Tennessee and Ohio before receiving scholarships to attend Brown University and pursue a Ph.D. in literature at Cambridge University. Sanders and his wife, Ruth, then settled in her hometown of Bloomington, Indiana, where he has taught for decades at Indiana University. Sanders has written short stories, novels, and science fiction but is best known for essays that center on experiences in his homeland and on recollections of youth. Acutely sensitive to the world's ills, Sanders has wrestled with the challenge of sustaining hope and joy in the face of increasing ecological degradation. His reflections on this paradox are evident in all his essay collections: *The Paradise of Bombs, Secrets of the Universe, Staying Put, Writing from the Center, Hunting for Hope,* and *The Force of Spirit.*

ALICE WALKER (1944–) grew up in rural Georgia, the seventh child in a sharecropper's family. She received scholarships to Tuskogee College and Sarah Lawrence University and completed her first book of poetry in her senior year of college. Walker lived for several years in the South and in New York City before settling permanently in California. Her adult years have been marked by vociferous social protest, advocating for the causes she holds dear—civil rights, solidarity with Central America and Cuba, the abolition of female circumcision, animal liberation, and care of the Earth. Among her numerous novels, books of poetry, and essays, the works that best depict her ecological conversion include *Anything We Love Can Be Saved, Living by the Word,* and *The Same River Twice.*

TERRY TEMPEST WILLIAMS (1955–) was raised in a Mormon household in Salt Lake City, Utah. Her early enthusiasm for untamed nature led her to study natural history and complete a master's degree in environmental education. Williams subsequently became staff naturalist for the Utah Museum of Natural History, working there for two decades before leaving to write full time. Williams's stories and books emphasize what she terms an "erotics of place"— a passionate relation to one's home ground. Her own bonds with the western deserts have drawn her into a more public and political role than her Mormon heritage sanctions, creating tensions within her family and community. The works that reveal most about Williams's turn to Earth are *Refuge, Desert Quartet, An Unspoken Hunger,* and *Red.*

The autobiographical stories of these primary writers reveal striking commonalities in experience despite marked differences in life circumstances. All six writers completed college, and five received graduate degrees. This level of formal education would be less noteworthy if they had grown up in middle-class homes with college-educated parents. However, four were raised by parents with little formal schooling and limited economic means. This fact counters the prevailing notion that nature (or ecological) writers are a privileged leisure class with time to reflect that working-class people cannot afford. The majority of these writers grew up in households with few material goods, ate out of subsistence gardens, and attended college on scholarships.

Despite limited economic means, these writers were privileged in nonmaterial ways. They had parents who, for all their foibles, were concerned with the welfare of their children. They also had access to untamed natural areas in youth and the freedom to explore those places (a theme developed in chapter 2).

Given their subsequent turns to Earth, it is worth noting that five of the six writers grew up in churchgoing families and four had a parent active in church leadership. Despite this early religious indoctrination (or perhaps because of it), none of the writers has maintained a strong church affiliation in adulthood. They reflect on their religious experiences in youth with some ambivalence, expressing appreciation tinged with anger and nostalgia for a potential never realized. The early influence of church may have helped open these writers to a spiritual outlook on life, a recognition of ineffable forces at work in the world. That conviction appears to have grown with time, even as their formal church ties have withered.

These writers occasionally draw on the teachings of childhood faiths or other spiritual traditions, but their primary sacral allegiance is to Earth. They do not identify themselves as spiritual hybrids, nor do they show any history of being serial converts, perennially seeking new forms of faith. Those who do label themselves spiritually choose unconventional descriptors, such as Terry Tempest Williams's term "naturalist" and Edward Abbey's appellation

"Earthiest." While standing firmly outside authoritarian and doctrinal institutions, few of them suggest that a spiritual concern for the Earth is fundamentally incompatible with institutional faiths. They neither discredit nor embrace the work of contemporary theologians who seek to reconcile doctrinal faiths with an Earth-based spirituality.

A wide range of variables beyond the religious sphere shape their turns to Earth—including gender, geographic setting, race, ethnicity, family, temperament, and personal bonds. Even within this small sampling of writers, I could not begin to account for how these variables affect the course of each person's conversion. I have noted only those factors whose influence is readily apparent (such as Momaday's Kiowa heritage or Carson's and Williams's unconventional family lives). I do not speculate on variables that the writers themselves don't directly address (such as the influence of gender or race on the conversion process). Such information would extend our understanding of ecological conversion, but it is beyond the scope of this preliminary exploration.

By highlighting commonalities among writers, this book risks masking the inevitable inconsistencies and ambiguities within each writer's life—making them seem like model ecological saints rather than flawed and fallible seekers. In an effort to more fairly portray the complexity of their experience, I do cite some of the writers' internal contradictions. However, the structure of a comparative study precludes a thorough exploration of all the tensions that mark each individual's ecological practice.

These writers are gifted at the art of narrative, but they are not exceptional in their spiritual or moral capacities. If they were extraordinary individuals, the patterns drawn from their narratives would be of limited value. Because they are fairly representative of the larger population (seemingly ordinary, complex people with an average share of foibles), their accounts of conversion become highly relevant, suggesting that a broader societal turn to Earth is possible.

Many of the converts described in this work participate in a loose-knit community of contemporary writers, artists, and local activists who share an ideal of ecological communion. Because its members are independent (tending to resist institutional ties), geographically dispersed, and nondoctrinal, this community cannot be termed an organized political or religious movement. There is no creed or mission statement binding them and few organizational links. Like many Native American populations, these individuals are joined by a reverence for the land: "Nature provides a language to express cosmology and belief: it forms the basis for understanding and practicing a way of life; it supplies materials for ritual symbolization; it draws together a community."[14]

Few members of this community have met in person, but they share in each other's lives through a fine and barely visible web of words. Increasingly these filamentary bonds are reinforced through regional workshops and national conferences that offer opportunities for individuals to plan, celebrate, and commiserate together. Terry Tempest Williams, one of the few writers to name this informal network, calls it the Coyote Clan. In Native American lore, coyote is the archetypal trickster whose chameleon nature embodies paradox. Coyote is profane and sacred, elusive and omnipresent, callous and compassionate, cultivated and wild. Williams envisions members of the Coyote Clan as having a similar tolerance for paradox, acknowledging the inherent contradictions in the world and in themselves.

The term *clan* seems an apt description for the affiliation among contemporary ecological writers. Clan suggests common origins, which these writers clearly share. They readily acknowledge their debt to literary forebears in the nature-writing tradition and to predecessors in oral cultures, the first people to shape stories on this continent. Clan also implies a sense of kinship, echoing the original meaning of ecology as home. All these writers see their familial households as belonging to the larger Earth household (which at present constitutes a troubled and broken home). They share in a desire to heal our ecological home through a broad societal transformation. The writers in this work are not bound by an ideology (in the doctrinal or political sense) so much as by idealism—a common commitment to transform the world. They seek to restore or, more aptly, to "re-story" a narrative lineage that links us to the natural whole. From their personal accounts of transformation, we may draw faith in the possibility of ecological renewal.

Elements of Ecological Conversion

"Bedrock," the opening chapter, explores the ecological conversion of writer Terry Tempest Williams—demonstrating how key elements of the process manifest in one individual's life story. A fifth-generation Mormon, Williams is devoted to her extended family and her home terrain in Utah. These bonds have shaped the path of her ecological turning through childhood experiences outdoors; familial mentors; revelatory encounters in the natural world; and a growing commitment to renew the land through story and ritual and defend it through local activism. The detailed profile of Williams's turn sets the context for subsequent chapters, each of which synthesizes material from numerous writers around a unifying theme. These thematic chapters all carry a title beginning with "R," an alliterative and mnemonic device that may prove helpful; other terms, though, could certainly substitute for those I have chosen.

"Remembrance," the second chapter, cites commonalities in the formative experiences of the primary writers—all of whom shared a strong affinity for the natural world as children, found support for this bond through mentors, and gained inspiration from the words and lives of established nature writers. The marked parallels in their experience suggest that contact with the natural world and with mentors (both familial and literary) may set the stage for a subsequent turn to Earth.

"Reflection," the third chapter, describes how periods of enforced introspection lead converts to reassess their place in the ecological whole. Psychic transformation can occur not only in response to deliberate immersion in natural settings but to experiences of loss, illness, estrangement, or despair. While reflective periods can prove emotionally taxing, they may awaken a sense of compassion that deepens an ecological practice.

"Revelation," the fourth chapter, illustrates how converts experience moments of insight that renew and reconstitute their lives. These profound glimpses into a larger mystery often affirm their sense of belonging to a sacred whole. Revelatory experiences can inspire fundamental changes in ecological belief and practice.

"Reciprocity," the fifth chapter, demonstrates how converts consciously strengthen their identification with other members of the ecological community. Writers often cultivate empathic modes of relation, seeking to counter the cultural taboos and engrained fears that separate humans from the rest of nature. A felt experience of reciprocity often fosters a stronger commitment to the ecological whole.

"Resistance," the sixth chapter, discusses how ecological converts—motivated by their deep affinity for the natural world—devote themselves to responsible action on its behalf. Some bear witness to environmental degradation primarily through writing; others take direct action through ecological restoration, land conservation, or civil disobedience. Their actions testify to a deepening bond with Earth.

"Ritual," the seventh chapter, portrays how creative and ritual arts support the conversion process. Through writing and sharing narratives and performing ceremonial rites, converts often affirm their sense of belonging within the natural world. Imaginative and sacred rituals become a means of simultaneously celebrating and renewing connections within the ecological community.

Each of the primary chapters ends with a section sketching aspects of my own turn to Earth. I hope that these reflections may prove useful as you trace your process of turning.

The elements of conversion recorded in this work are descriptive rather than prescriptive. They do not constitute a "how to" guide or moral doctrine; rather, they map the outlines of a complex transformational process and suggest patterns that warrant further attention. Because this work marks the first attempt to describe a model of inner ecological transformation, its findings are necessarily preliminary—neither comprehensive nor conclusive. Even among the six primary writers, each individual does not appear to experience every element (certainly not to the same degree). Different patterns dominate the conversion narratives of each writer. Yet there is, amidst the variability, a surprising degree of commonality.

The patterns evident in the following chapters can be likened to models depicting more conventional forms of religious conversion. Scholars James Loder, Lewis Rambo, and Paul Brockelman suggest that conversion is a complex, dynamic process that can be viewed in terms of distinct stages. The stages are not wholly discrete but are "paradoxically *both* chronological *and* simultaneous."[15]

Rambo identifies seven stages of conversion: context, crisis, quest, encounter, interaction, commitment, and consequences.[16] Loder cites five steps: conflict-in-context; interlude for scanning; insight felt with intuitive force; release and repatterning; and interpretation and verification.[17] Brockelman describes seven stages of spiritual transformation: awareness of nonbeing; religious longing; interpretive vision; spiritual commitment; mystical experience and existential transformation; spiritual integration; and compassionate love and caring.[18]

The stages in these models of spiritual transformation share clear thematic ties with elements of ecological conversion. For example, *resistance* coincides with the category of commitment outlined by Rambo and Brockelman, and *revelation* parallels Brockelman's stage of "mystical experience" and Loder's "insight felt with intuitive force." The pattern of *reflection* evident among ecological writers can be likened to the stage that involves a "quest," "interlude for scanning," or "religious longing."

The process of turning to Earth, though, resists sequential modeling where one stage routinely follows another. It involves elements (distinguishable parts of a larger whole) or patterns (recurrent themes or characteristics) rather than discrete steps in a linear journey. Ecological conversion can best be seen as a dynamic mobile, in which each element circles at its own pace—moving intermittently at times, but always in tandem with other elements.

As the mobile metaphor suggests, conversion is not a singular, discrete event but an ongoing process. The testimony of ecological converts supports Thomas Merton's assertion that "we are not converted only once in our lives but many times."[19] The convert's path is one of "permanent revolution."[20]

This revolutionary perspective challenges the classical vision of conversion as a means to spiritual certitude, a serene inner state unruffled by concerns of the material world. Psychologist William James reports that conversion commonly fosters visions, ecstatic happiness, and a sense of the world transfigured.[21] Seeing conversion as a path to nirvana, though, can distort both the process (by portraying it as a form of spiritual self-help) and the outcome (by overlooking the demands of a lived practice). Ecological conversion offers no haven of spiritual bliss apart from the destruction ravaging the natural world. It does not lead people *out* of the world but deeper and deeper *into* it.

Every turn to Earth is fraught with the dynamic tension of polarities that cannot be reconciled: the necessity of death to nourish life; the acute fragility and resilience of natural systems; the cycles of scarcity and abundance; and the stability that inheres within constant change. These paradoxes in outer ecology mirror ones within. Many converts find themselves challenged to embrace life in the face of relentless loss; to distinguish sufficiency from surfeit; and to cultivate the strength to be vulnerable.

Tensions generated by these paradoxes can prove overwhelming. Writer Terry Tempest Williams speaks for many ecological converts in asking, "where do we find the strength not to be pulled apart by our passions?"[22] The question is far from rhetorical. There are times, some writers admit, when they are torn asunder by the polarities. Despite this struggle, they resist the false promise that paradoxes can be effectively resolved. There is no chapter on *resolution* among the elements of conversion outlined here. Converts learn that the discipline of an ecological practice entails holding the poles together, knowing there can be no lasting reconciliation. They rely on art to help them negotiate the great fecundity and friction of a life intimately bound to the ecological whole.

An Invitation

This book interweaves findings and insights from many disciplines and is not confined—in form or language—by the protocol of a particular field. It represents a narrative tapestry rather than a conventional scholarly treatise. I hope it will prove engaging and inspiring to environmental professionals and scholars of all stripes, as well as to citizens concerned with the fate of the Earth.

The chapters that follow explore the mysterious and dynamic realm of inner ecology. Several dozen writer-guides help to bush-whack through this uncharted terrain, revealing the contours of a landscape that may feel at once familiar and foreign. You are invited to join in the reconnaissance. I hope that the ground you cover and the stories you hear will inspire your turn to Earth.

1

Bedrock

One Writer's Path

The enterprise of conservation is a
revolution, an evolution of the spirit.

—Terry Tempest Williams,
An Unspoken Hunger

In turning to Earth, writers travel different paths yet cover common ground. Subsequent chapters map this shared terrain, drawing on the life narratives of diverse individuals. Here we attend to one writer's story, seeing how ecological conversion defines the experience of writer Terry Tempest Williams.

Williams's story helps to illustrate the dynamic interplay of factors—internal and external, deliberate and unplanned, individual and communal—that shape the course of a turn to Earth. Looking at these patterns in one individual reveals the complexity and variability of the transformational process.

Each subsequent chapter discusses a single element of ecological conversion, interweaving stories from many individuals. This collective view helps to depict each element from different vantage points, giving us a broader perspective on the conversion process. Yet it makes the interweaving of patterns within each life somewhat harder to discern. The opening portrait of Williams may help to underscore those linkages through subsequent chapters.

Conversion to Earth, for Williams, involves a spiraling process of turning and re-turning. She continuously draws upon past experiences and insights to amplify and deepen her perspective in the present. Her roots lie deep in the Great Basin region of Utah, homeland to her family for five generations. Experiences outdoors and time with mentors have nourished her passionate link to the land, inspiring a growing commitment to political activism. They have helped her relinquish patterns that once defined her—orthodox tenets of Mormonism, traditional roles and rules for women, and puritanical inhibitions about sensual experience. Each person, Williams believes, carries a "huge cloak of conditioning": the challenge lies in shedding those layers to discover what lies at the core.[1]

Her inspiration in this quest comes from her homeland, a region eroded by strong winds and flash floods and cracked open by frost and parching heat. The desert is a potent metaphor for relinquishment, Williams explains, because "what is essential remains and everything else is washed away."[2] She strives to model her inner ecology after the desert ecosystem, letting go of old habits and assumptions and attending carefully to what she terms the "bedrock self."

Bedrock imagery recurs frequently in Williams's narratives and in works by other ecological writers. In geological terms, bedrock is the stratum closest to the molten heart of Earth, the volcanic center of creative power. It is foundational yet nearly fluid. Metaphorically, bedrock represents the ground that supports one's deepest convictions. Edward Abbey claims to take his stand on a "bedrock of animal faith," placing ultimate trust in the regenerative capacity of the elemental Earth.[3] Stable ground also can lie within: Scott Russell Sanders describes his need to dig "down to some bedrock of feeling and belief," a place close to the dynamic core of his being.[4]

Williams sees the bedrock self as joining inner and outer ecology, fusing each individual to a larger web of being. Just as geological bedrock is not reducible, one's bedrock identity is an indivisible part of a vast whole. This perspective dissolves the long-standing philosophical divide between self and surroundings, opening the way, in one scholar's words, to "the possibility of being simultaneously ego- and eco-centric, individuated and integrated, and—once and for all—both human and 'natural.'"[5]

The melding of self with the larger whole can lead to spiritual enlightenment. Williams sees bedrock as "solid, expansive, full of light and originality," reflecting the existence of an inner light within each being.[6] In her view, a spark of the divine fires the creative core of our lives.

The light of that bedrock self appears when surface layers erode, suggesting that loss may be essential to the transformational process. A deeper commitment to Earth, Williams finds, requires a protracted process of excavation. She digs down toward bedrock through accumulated layers of familial history, religious indoctrination, and cultural socialization. In the course of this excavation, Williams lets go of comforting beliefs and traditions as well as constricting dictates. Some losses are liberating; others go unredeemed. Turning to Earth, for Williams, demands a consistent practice of relinquishment: she enters fully into the process, convinced that change works inexorably on every individual whether or not one resists. "Nobody escapes life," Williams holds: "one way or another it erodes you."[7]

Remembrance

Long before she formed words to express it, Williams forged a bond with the land. Etched in her memory are indelible images from the landscapes of youth: the mountains around Jackson Hole, Wyoming; the scrub oak terrain of the Wasatch foothills; the briny shallows of Great Salt Lake.

Williams recalls hiking up to a waterfall in Wyoming when she was four, supported by her mother and grandmother holding each hand. At the water's edge, they lowered her to drink from the clear pool. It was, Williams reflects, "an initiation into this fountain of knowledge, spirituality, vitality, life, curiosity."[8] This early baptism into the source of life—both real and metaphoric—prompted Williams to seek spiritual sustenance in the natural world. For her, the pure mountain pool held the soul's elixir that Robert Frost describes in his poem "Directive": "Here are your waters and your watering place. Drink and be whole again beyond confusion."[9]

Williams takes her directive from the sacred sites of youth. She visits them to recapture a baptismal sense of immersion in nature. There is, she believes, "a constant communion and sacrament that we have to go back to again and again . . . to renew our vows, if you will."[10] Religious metaphors underscore the spiritual quality of Williams's kinship with the natural world. Her "vows" to follow an ecological practice are renewed through sacramental moments of communion outdoors, times when she is made whole again beyond confusion. Earth is the wellspring that feeds her ecological conscience and activism.

Family members, particularly her beloved grandmother Kathryn Blackett Tempest, fostered Williams's early devotion to place. Mimi (as she was known to family) assumed the mentoring role that Rachel Carson describes in *The Sense of Wonder*: "If a child is to keep alive his inborn sense of wonder, . . . he needs the companionship of at least one adult who can share it, rediscovering with him the joy, excitement and mystery of the world we live in."[11] Mimi gave Williams her first field guide to birds at age five and routinely took her on hikes and ornithological outings.

She also introduced her granddaughter to mythological and spiritual dimensions of the natural world. During Williams's childhood, Mimi read her way clear of the Mormon orthodoxy, immersing herself in psychological and spiritual works by such writers as Carl Jung, Krishnamurti and Marie-Louise von Franz. Through Mimi's example, Williams learned to question established doctrines and cultivate faith in her own perspectives. Mimi's subversive spirituality gave Williams an alternative constellation of values and beliefs in the midst of a conservative orthodox culture. Williams notes that since her parents were strict adherents to Mormonism in those years, "the tutelage of my childhood really rested in the arms of my grandparents."[12]

Alongside their orthodox practice, her immediate family held a deep appreciation for the natural world. All four Tempest children were encouraged to play outdoors in the Wasatch foothills that lay beyond their home in Salt Lake City. Williams credits her father with introducing her to the physical world, taking her hiking, swimming, and hunting, and teaching her about native soils and landforms.

She gained further encouragement to bond with the land by reading classics of environmental writing during adolescence. Works by Henry Thoreau, Aldo Leopold, and Rachel Carson introduced her to new philosophical and political views and impressed on her the strength and grace of lives governed by a strong ecological conscience. These literary mentors proved inspirational, reinforcing Williams's love for the land and her sense of moral responsibility. Their words became her "sacred text."[13]

Williams's intellectual horizons stretched further at age eighteen when she attended a program at the Teton Science School in Wyoming. The school's director, Ted Major, was the first Democrat she ever recalls meeting. His emphasis on asking questions and entertaining new perspectives proved revolutionary: "that experience," Williams reflects, "opened a door in me that I could never close again."[14] Through two subsequent summers at the Teton Science School, she strengthened her skills as a naturalist and her conviction that environmental work represented her vocational calling.

The school introduced Williams to a supportive community of naturalists and writers (such as Marty Murie, Barry Lopez, and Gary Snyder) who shared her passion for the land. From them, Williams drew inspiration to venture into new personal and professional terrain. The question "do I dare?" became her mantra during those years: "Do I dare go get a master's degree in environmental education so I can share this? Do I dare go to the Navajo reservation and really look at this other culture? . . . Do I dare take a real job [at the Museum of Natural History]? No woman in my family had ever held a job."[15]

Williams's courage to venture beyond established bounds was amply rewarded. The ecological awakening that began at the Teton Science School intensified during her year teaching on a Navajo reservation. The rich lessons of that time, documented in *Pieces of White Shell*, reverberate through her later works. Immersion in an oral culture that was deeply attuned to the land reconstituted Williams's own sense of language, listening, and belonging. It gave her a profound appreciation for the power of narrative and the value of having strong roots.

Having grown up in a homogeneous Mormon community, Williams found the diverse perspectives she encountered among the Navajo both challenging and enlightening. She gained an abiding respect for contemporary tribal people and their ancestral bonds with the land. The experience prompted an ecological coming-of-age, helping Williams to recognize the importance of natural interconnections and diverse cultural values and practices.

Williams continues to be nourished by the spiritual springs that fed her early life. She still lives in the Utah desert, close to extended family. She undertakes pilgrimages to the settings of her early initiation into the larger natural world. She wears the turquoise jewelry her grandmother Mimi wore, a symbolic link to the spirit of her most influential mentor. She returns to the sacred texts that helped inspire her turning. And she continues to learn the language and culture of native inhabitants (crafting, for example, a libretto that honors a local mountain in the language of the native Ute tribe). For Williams, the art of remembrance is not a passive or nostalgic gesture but a means of engaging the full depth of one's being in the moment. The present must incorporate the past, she believes, even as both give way to the future. Williams relies on her writing to hold the whole together. She sees her stories as "an attempt to heal myself, to confront what I do not know, to create a path for myself with the idea that 'memory is the only way home.'"[16]

Reflection

Williams recalls her childhood passing in a predictable succession of seasons and birthdays until her fifteenth year. Then that stable pattern shattered. Her mother was diagnosed with breast cancer and underwent surgery. The cancer went into remission, but Williams never regained a sense of security. Death was no longer an abstraction but a felt presence in her daily life. It brought a heightened sense of immediacy and intensity to all she did: "I've never felt that I had the luxury of putting things off," she explains: "all of a sudden, life [came] acutely into focus."[17]

When her mother's cancer returned twelve years later, Williams was swept into a prolonged period of grief and relinquishment. Through four years darkened by the impending deaths of her mother and grandmothers, she struggled to find meaning amidst loss. Her anguish was deepened by the simultaneous flooding of the Bear River Migratory Bird Sanctuary along Great Salt Lake, a natural refuge that had long given her spirit solace. Record-level rains caused the lake to rise, depriving migratory birds of the fertile marshlands they had frequented.

Williams felt displaced and disoriented as the cornerstones of her identity—family and nature—washed out beneath her. Navigating through a landscape void of familiar bearings, she saw her life come to pivot on the question of how we find refuge in change: "I am slowly, painfully discovering that my refuge is not found in my mother, my grandmother, or even the birds of Bear River. My refuge exists in my capacity to love. If I can learn to love death then I can begin to find refuge in change."[18]

Williams's poignant sense of life's fragility intensified as she realized her own health was at risk. Because of exposure to atmospheric radiation (from above-ground atomic tests conducted in the western desert), Williams may not escape the fate of her mother and grandmothers. Nine women in her family have contracted cancer, and seven have died from it. Williams has been told by her oncologist, "it is not if you get cancer, but when."[19]

Williams has faced her fear of death by holding herself close to relatives in the dying process: "I cared for them, bathed their scarred bodies, . . . held their foreheads as they vomited green-black bile, and . . . shot them with morphine when the pain became inhuman."[20] Through this grueling experience, Williams comes to honor death on its terms, discovering dignity amidst the destruction. When she encounters a whistling swan that has recently died, she consciously attends to the bird, straightening its body and smoothing its feathers. Through patient care and imagination, Williams brings warmth to the cold anonymity of its death:

> I looked for two black stones, found them, and placed them over the eyes like coins. They held. And, using my own saliva as my mother and grandmother had done to wash my face, I washed the swan's black bill and feet until they shone like patent leather.
>
> I have no idea of the amount of time that passed in preparation of the swan. What I remember most is lying next to its body and imagining the great white bird in flight."[21]

Through this act, Williams delves into grief until finding the grace within it.

Encounters with death lead Williams into a realm where contradictory forces are inseparably joined. Beauty cannot be found apart from destruction or stability apart from change. She comes to see paradox as defining the contours of both inner and outer ecology. Her home terrain reminds her that opposing qualities can be held together. Williams views Great Salt Lake as an embodiment of paradox, calling it "the liquid lie of the West."[22] It is wilderness by the city, a vast oasis in the desert that cannot be drunk, with waters both tame and treacherous. Dwelling literally and figuratively on the shores of paradox allows Williams to face loss and suffering without despair, and even without hope. She learns that hope can feed denial, obstructing one's capacity for change. Hope seeks a different outcome—the remission of cancer, a permanent cure, life over death. To relinquish hope, though, can be a spiritual challenge, as T. S. Eliot observed: "I said to my soul, be still, and wait without hope. For hope would be hope for the wrong thing . . . there is yet faith. But the faith and the love and the hope are all in the waiting."[23] Like Eliot, Williams concludes that one must let go hope and abide in faith, a conviction of meaning in things as they are. "Better a cruel truth," Edward Abbey counseled, "than a comfortable delusion."[24]

Confronting death directly and persistently has deepened Williams's commitment to live mindfully in the present and to reconsider truths and norms she once accepted. Raised with admonitions not to "make waves" or "rock the boat," she spent years muzzling herself in a "culture that rarely asks questions because it has all the answers."[25] Williams abandoned this passive stance after recognizing that the cancer epidemic in her family and community could be due to silent complicity in governmental actions that threaten public health. Her grandmother Mimi helped propel Williams toward more outspoken resistance. Williams visited her grandmother in the hospital during Mimi's final bout with cancer, just after her grandmother had experienced laborlike pains and passed a bloody, malignant tumor. Mimi told her granddaughter: "when I looked into the water closet and saw what my body had expelled, the first thought that came into my mind was 'Finally, I am rid of the orthodoxy.' My advice to you, dear, is do it consciously."[26] Williams chose to heed her grandmother's counsel.

Revelation

In stepping away from religious orthodoxy, Williams has come to trust convictions born of experience. Her ecological practice is nourished by her sensual immersion in the natural world. Through attunement to her surroundings, Williams attains revelatory glimpses into a wider spiritual sphere. Her faith in mystical connection comes in part from the teachings of family and church. As a child she was encouraged to look beyond surface appearances. Her father, a pipeline contractor who works with geologic substrates, repeatedly cautioned her that "nothing is as it appears."[27] From her grandmother Mimi, Williams learned of depth psychology and the potential power of dreams and intuitive insights. Even the Mormon faith of her youth held a sense of the fantastical, affirming the individual's power to hear voices and have visions. In keeping with that tradition, Williams did have a vision at age seventeen after two days of prayer and fasting on a remote ranch. Ironically, though, the vision affirmed her reliance on internal truth over church doctrine.

Williams no longer couches her appreciation for mystery in conventional deistic terms. She refers instead to the need for "coyote consciousness," a recognition that life runs far deeper than what is visible at the surface. Williams sees the spiritual realm as rife with surprise: she values the way life improvises. There is a trickster quality in the natural world and in us that Williams trusts for its very fickleness.

Dreams can reveal the mystery that lurks, coyotelike, in the shadows beneath consciousness. Just before being told of her mother's ovarian cancer, Williams dreamed that she was in imminent danger, hiding under her grandmother's bed as black helicopters approached the house. Similar premonitions come to her in waking. She terms them "moments of peripheral perceptions . . . short, sharp flashes of insight we tend to discount."[28]

There are even times when dreams and reality merge. For decades, Williams was plagued by a recurrent nightmare in which a blinding light burned over the desert's mesas. Williams recounted this dream to her father after her mother died. He replied that Williams *had* witnessed such an explosion during an atomic bomb test in 1957 (when she was two). Sitting on her mother's lap during a drive through Nevada, Williams had seen a gold-stemmed mushroom cloud light the sky as the ground shook and radioactive ash sifted down on their car.

The revelation that her nightmare was real incensed Williams, converting her private grief into a fierce commitment to political activism. Further research confirmed that her family's high incidence of cancer could result from their being downwind of atomic blasts planned and orchestrated by the federal government. "It was at this moment," she recounts, "that I realized the deceit I had been living under. . . . [Now] I must question everything, even if it means losing my faith."[29]

Williams's faith has also been challenged and reconstituted by encounters with what she terms the "immediacy of life, even in death."[30] The most profound revelation occurred as she witnessed her mother's passage into death. Williams sat by her mother's side, holding her hand and breathing in unison with her: "Faint breaths. Soft breaths. In my heart I say 'Let go . . . let go . . . follow the light.' . . . There is a crescendo of movement, like walking up a pyramid of light. And it is sexual, the concentration of love, of being fully present. Pure feeling. Pure color. I can feel her spirit rising through the top of her head. Her eyes focus on mine with total joy—a fullness that transcends words."[31] This experience transformed Williams's sense of the spiritual, making it more engaged and relational, or what she terms erotic. In her view, the erotic involves an intimate bodily immersion in the world—a felt experience of natural cycles and elemental being. "It's that notion of surrendering to something greater than ourselves," Williams explains. "The erotic is about love, our deep hunger for communion."[32] Williams views the erotic in both sensual and sexual terms. It represents a passionate connection in which heart, body, and mind join with the spirit and matter of the natural world.

Williams believes that an erotic connection to the cycles of life and death can provide serenity in the midst of turbulence. Given life's mystical peaks and painful troughs, she seeks a spiritual equilibrium that will allow her "to be present in those waves and emotional tides but to possess a solidarity of soul."[33]

Williams holds this spiritual balance best when in contact with the natural world. She feels most grounded outdoors, particularly in her desert homeland and around Great Salt Lake. On its windblown shores, Williams attests to how she is "spun, supported, and possessed by the spirit who dwells here. Great Salt Lake is a spiritual magnet that will not let me go. Dogma doesn't hold me. Wildness does."[34] In such revelatory moments, Williams affirms that her spiritual bond to Earth is not mediated by words or institutions. The experience of communion is the only evidence she needs that spirit infuses the elemental world.

Reciprocity

Williams cultivates an engagement with place that emphasizes bodily connection: "I believe our most poignant lessons come through the body, the skin, the cells," she asserts: "it is through the body we feel the world, both its pain and its beauty."[35] Her physical bond with Earth is made manifest in *Desert Quartet: An Erotic Landscape,* a work recounting intimate encounters with elemental matter. In crafting this piece, Williams explains, she sought to shape a text "born out of the body, not out of the mind. So in a sense you feel it before you comprehend it. Which is what I think happens when we go into the land."[36] The rituals described in *Desert Quartet* seem to grow spontaneously from the physical and spiritual union of person and place. They reflect what Williams claims she most loves and fears: passion. Only through opening our bodily selves to the natural whole, she believes, can we grasp the extent of our spiritual connection: "To restrain our passionate nature in the face of a generous life" is a form of spiritual deprivation.[37]

A passionate, embodied connection to place can shape our moral relation to the whole. "Through an erotics of place," Williams asserts, "our sensitivity becomes our sensibility."[38] A spiritual, aesthetic, and emotional bond with the land can nourish a sense of moral responsibility: the more joyful one's experience of place, the more fiercely one must defend it. Although some ethicists might dispute this link, it fairly reflects Williams's experience. Her passionate love for the land continually renews her commitment to act on its behalf.

Williams strengthens her erotic connection to place through time spent alone outdoors, attending to other forms of life. She experiences these "solitary" times as deeply relational. To better enter into a sustained dialogue with the land, Williams cultivates the art of listening. She credits her Mormon upbringing with teaching her to listen to elders, and Navajo culture with teaching her to hear the many voices of Earth. By quieting down, Williams suggests, individuals can attune themselves to other beings and the spirit of place: "what I love about the natural world and absolutely rely on," she reflects, "is stillness. Where you can sit and it enlarges your heart."[39] Such conscious centering can heighten spiritual receptivity by awakening wonder and awe. Williams's focus on sensory wakefulness has come to inform her understanding of prayer. As a child, she thought prayer involved talking to God. Now she understands it more as a form of listening, opening to the countless forms and dimensions of being.

A felt sense of kinship with the natural whole can inspire conservation, in Williams's view: "If people have a relationship to the land, I believe they will do everything within their means and power to protect it. Because it becomes family and people will defend their families."[40] An intimate bond with the land, she concedes, is not without tension. Ties within human families can become charged and challenging as relations stretch to encompass other species. Defending the threatened desert tortoise has brought Williams into direct conflict with her own clan, many of whom work in the family's construction business—laying pipeline and conduit across the desert. Her relatives chafe against governmental strictures supporting the tortoise and against the "enviros" like Williams who intervene on behalf of the ancient reptile. In response, Williams strives to listen with compassion to her family members of all species and to learn, in Breyten Breytenbach's words, "the slow art of revolutionary patience."[41]

Despite these inherent tensions, Williams relishes the paradox that accompanies interdependence—the demands and rewards of being inescapably bound in community. Her tolerance for conflict allows her to pursue visions for ecological change even within her native community, a conservative Mormon enclave.

Resistance

Williams counts herself a "member of a border tribe" among Mormons, separated by the chasm between her Earth-centered spirituality and orthodox church tenets.[42] She values the communal strength and high ideals of Mormon culture but no longer abides by its religious tenets or gender roles. Her independence, outspoken feminism, and commitment to creative expression counter Mormon norms dictating that women be docile mothers, devoting their creative energies to child rearing.

Williams's choice to forego motherhood has incited scorn and derision among some Mormons. She notes that "the most threatening and subversive aspect of *Refuge* wasn't talking about a Heavenly Mother, . . . [or] about power or hierarchical structure. . . . It was the aspect that Brooke and I don't have children."[43] One scholarly critic, herself a Mormon woman, suggests that because Williams rejects "the ultimate Mormon woman's experience: childbirth," she cannot claim to be a midwife to her mother's soul (in attending her death) and is only suited to be "midwife to a dead flock [of sheep]."[44] Conforming to cultural roles, the Mormon critic implies, is an essential prerequisite to any spiritual experience.

While stepping away from such rigid orthodoxies, Williams maintains a strong sense of religious devotion. Her spiritual allegiance to Earth fuels a commitment to write and act on its behalf, countering the broader culture. "It is the desert that persuades me toward love," she attests, "to step outside and defy custom one more time."[45] Love calls forth a moral response that prompts Williams to challenge societal norms, opening her to censure from family members, community acquaintances, and total strangers. Even within one's own community, she reports, "you're not understood, or you're misunderstood, or you're projected upon because you represent the breaking of taboo."[46] She concedes that such judgments are painful, but they fail to erode her moral commitment to honor the larger web of life.

Williams has testified before Congress on several occasions, spoken at political rallies, served on the boards of environmental organizations, and helped spearhead major legislative campaigns. In all these political acts, she strives to incorporate her aesthetic, spiritual, and moral sensibilities. For example, Williams co-edited a chapbook on Utah's wildlands for members of Congress as a means of affirming "the power of story to bypass political rhetoric and pierce the heart."[47] In civil disobedience actions at the Nevada nuclear testing site, she has engaged in group dancing, drumming, and singing. She perceives no innate conflict between creative expression and political acts: both serve to honor one's connections to Earth.

Williams holds great faith in the potential of what she terms "responsive citizenry," the capacity ordinary individuals have to effect change and improve social and environmental conditions. While conceding that this country's democratic potential is far from being realized (due in part to concentrations of power), Williams believes that citizens can still effect change if they "choose to be sufficiently outraged."[48]

Over the years, the focus of her political resistance has shifted from national to local efforts. She now takes more satisfaction and challenge in grassroots work done close to home—projects such as a course co-taught with a community gardener for underprivileged girls; a "nature school" held for neighborhood children; and local land trust initiatives. By contributing to community life at this scale, Williams suggests, we do our required "home work" in the places we love, making "certain all is not destroyed under the banner of progress, expediency, or ignorance."[49]

Balancing the call of engaged citizenship with the solitude that writing demands has proven challenging. Williams long ago relinquished the vision of a writing life apart from the tumult of politics. Yet it is a constant struggle for her to accommodate both "the obligations of a public life and the spiritual necessity of a private one."[50] To help maintain this balance, Williams structures her life by the seasons. Spring and fall are times for travel—teaching, lecturing, and political work. Winter is hibernation time, a season of solitude and quiet for writing. Summer is devoted to family and time in the natural world. This cyclic pattern helps Williams define her limits and live within them.

In her practice of societal resistance, Williams gains sustenance from knowing that she belongs to a broad network of individuals who are "quietly subversive on behalf of the land."[51] Williams portrays members of this clan as impassioned, reflecting her view that an ecological practice requires not just commitment but exuberance. The best means to honor our essential interdependence, she holds, is to celebrate those connections through creative and ritual arts.

Ritual

Writing helps Williams touch bedrock—the molten core of her creativity—and bring forth that passion to share with others. Her narratives seem to inspire a similar quest among readers, prompting them to dig deep and reflect on their truest sources of vitality.

The act of writing and sharing stories, Williams believes, can strengthen one. It has offered her a path of integrity amidst wrenching life paradoxes—being "a radical soul in a conservative religion," a woman devoted to family with no children of her own, a writer who cherishes privacy and solitude yet is compelled to acts of public testimony.[52] Creative writing helps Williams navigate through contradictory forces to find what Thomas Merton termed "the hidden wholeness that lies beneath the broken surface of our lives."[53] The surface contradictions may never be reconciled, but imaginative and ritual arts reveal a larger unity.

Williams envisions creative ritual as the "formulas by which harmony is restored."[54] The world is animated, she believes, and certain rituals and obligations are needed to acknowledge those spirits. She recalls having had—even as a child—an "incapacitating sense of ritual" that went far beyond her family's Mormon practices. Williams sensed that ritual was a means of "reciprocity with the gods," a way to enter into dialogue with other dimensions of being.[55] To open this exchange, one must look for opportunities to acknowledge the movement of spirit in the world. Williams finds many of these in her explorations outdoors. Often her rituals are spontaneous and evolving responses to the character of a particular moment and place—such as bathing in a river at sunrise or forming figurines from native clay.

In a culture of fragmentation and estrangement, rituals can help bind humans back into the larger web of life. Williams favors the resurgence of communal celebrations that honor the shifting seasons and returning wildlife, affirming our essential interdependence. Too many established rituals, she believes, have grown vacuous. Williams felt this void acutely when she faced the deaths of family members and needed meaningful rituals to support her through a time of unprecedented loss. She had to create her own because the culture offered farcical exercises that denied death, rather than helping her come to terms with its powerful reality. When her mother died, Williams rebelled against the funeral home procedures that robbed her mother's carapace of dignity: "I stood . . . enraged at our inability to let the dead be dead," she writes. "And I wept over the hollowness of our rituals." That experience led her to revitalize desiccated rituals and create new means of celebrating bonds with the Earth.

An ecological practice, for Williams, is not a static set of routines but an ongoing improvisation. It engages all one's creative and political energy into what is both a lived art and a spiritual discipline. She cherishes her links to the past and the grounding power of tradition but has learned the spiritual necessity of relinquishment. The paradoxical pull between conservation and change is one of many contradictions within which she dwells. Her ecological practice pivots on paradox: the counterbalance of opposing forces and cycles helps center her in the midst of flux.

Williams maintains an equilibrium by continually reaffirming her erotic attachment to home ground. Her spiritual bond with the land takes form in an embodied practice that is—at once—creative, moral, and political. Turning to Earth consciously and unequivocally, Williams takes action even in the face of uncertainty. The challenge, she maintains, is not to retreat into dogma but to be satisfied without answers, trusting in the open-ended nature of life: "Our dreams of safety must disappear," she writes. "The mountain we love is the mountain we fear / Leap before you look—."[57]

2

Remembrance

The remembrance of childhood is a long remembrance, and
the incidents often make milestones in a personal history.
— Ellen Glasgow, *The Woman Within*

I have climbed into silence trying for clear air
and seen the peaks rising above me like the gods.
That is where they live, the old people say.
I used to hear them speak when I was a child . . .

Lately I write, trying to combine sound and memory,
searching for that significance once heard and nearly lost.
— Paula Gunn Allen, "Recuerdo"

Early experiences outdoors hold a depth of meaning that can reverberate in one throughout life. Children readily immerse themselves
in the natural world, saturating their senses in the elements. They
splash gleefully through mud puddles, bury into leaf piles, and
roll in snow, free of the inhibitions that come with age. Place per-
meates them, imprinting on heart and mind. "Human imagination
is shaped," writer Barry Lopez observes, "by the architecture of the
world it encounters at an early age."[1] For many ecological writers,
that architecture comprised intimate and accessible natural areas;

relatives and mentors to guide their explorations outdoors; and books and stories about lives in the wild. These early influences set the direction of their turns to Earth.

Conscious acts of remembrance can reawaken a long dormant sense of belonging to the natural whole, an intimate connection experienced before our identities calcified in adulthood. These recollections can dissolve the accumulated barriers that divide us from the outer world and our own bedrock depths. Through the process of ecological conversion, a narrowly bounded sense of self can give way to a more inclusive identity.

This pervasive sense of interconnection is hard to label or describe because it challenges the Western concept of identity as defined by ego or physical form. Norwegian philosopher Arne Naess, a pioneer of the deep ecology movement, refers to it as the "Ecological Self" (a self not discrete from the broader natural community), while Buddhist monk Thich Nhat Hanh terms it "interbeing." An expanded self can more readily identify with other creatures and the elemental world. Scott Momaday describes the change as a horizontal mode of perception, "an extension of . . . awareness across the whole landscape." A wide-angle view of the land and its life-forms places humans within the context of the ecological whole so that a person's "idea of himself comprehends his relationship to the land."[2]

This inclusive ecological identity often traces back to childhood experiences outdoors. The writers featured in this book spent extensive time in the natural world during youth. Their explorations covered a diverse range of habitats from desert tracts and farm regions to heavily used and even abused landscapes. Whatever the character of their native terrain, these writers attest to the enduring imprint of place.

The years of middle childhood (from ages six to twelve) are an important period for bonding with Earth, according to educators and developmental psychologists. During this time, children begin actively exploring their immediate surroundings and cultivating empathy for other beings. They make themselves at home in the natural world, building forts, dens, and tree houses and creating elaborate maps of their local environs. Scott Russell Sanders characterizes this childhood terrain as "the landscape you learn before you retreat inside the illusion of your skin."[3]

Being less constrained than adults by an ego-bound sense of self, children often grasp ecological linkages intuitively. They can enter fully into the gestalt of place, feeling the wholeness of the world through all their senses. Scott Momaday, for example, recalls the permeable identity he experienced riding horseback as a child: "After a time the horse became an extension of my senses, touching me to the earth, the air, and the sun more perfectly than I could touch these things for myself. Separate creatures though we were, there were moments when there was practically no telling us apart. We were one whole and distinct image in the plane—indeed more than an image, an entity of substance."[4] Momaday and his horse, once discrete beings, dissolve into a dynamic pattern of relation so strong that they become essentially one unit.

Such a fusion of self and environs can profoundly affect a child's identity, providing what psychologist Edith Cobb calls "a revelatory sense of continuity—an immersion of [the] whole organism in the outer world of forms, colors, and motions."[5] This fluid exchange between outer and inner ecology may be what allows the natural world to imprint so deeply on children's imaginations. Cobb suggests that these vivid experiences are universal among children and can be consciously fostered by adults (as the stories in chapter 4 demonstrate).

Moments when inner and outer ecology merge can give rise to lasting visions and dreams. Many ecological writers attribute their spiritual beliefs to early experiences outdoors that sparked their imaginations and evoked an enduring sense of awe. Terry Tempest Williams describes her native desert terrain as a setting that "turns us into believers."[6] Its humbling power and paradoxical nature continually reinforce her early conviction that the miraculous abides within the everyday world. One need not go in search of the sacred, Williams holds: "By being out in the land . . . one is simply standing in the center of it."[7]

Even those who resist naming the divine acknowledge the enduring impact that early bonds with the natural world have on their spiritual growth. Edward Abbey, who disavowed doctrinal religion, could still write: "my deepest emotions—those so deep they lie closer to music than to words—were formed, somehow, by intimate association in childhood with the woods on the hill, the stream that flowed through the pasture . . . the sugar maples, the hayfields."[8] The primal sense of connection to the land that marked Abbey's youth grew into a lifelong sense of kinship, propelling his turn to Earth.

Alice Walker also draws inspiration from her early spiritual empathy with other beings. For many years, she lost that intimate sense of connection before discovering "there is a very thin membrane, human-adult-made, that separates us from this seemingly vanished world, where plants and animals still speak a language we humans understand."[9] Peeling back that membrane, Walker finds intact her childhood sense of an animate world. This discovery renews her compassion for other beings and her resolve to protect the Earth.

The First Essential Adaptation

Bonding with place can represent a process of mythic dimensions: "there can be the matching of your own nature with this gorgeous nature of the land," scholar Joseph Campbell suggests: "it is the first essential adaptation."[10] The terrain of home imprints on the imagination, coming to shape our most basic modes of perception and expression. Poet Joy Harjo believes the effects of this early imprinting can be felt for decades. She traces her identity back to time spent bonding with the soil of her home ground: "When I was a little kid in Oklahoma I would get up before everyone else and go outside to a place of dark rich earth next to the foundation of the house. I would dig piles of earth with a stick, smell it, form it. It had sound. Maybe that's when I learned to write poetry."[11] Contact with native soil awakened Harjo's capacity to listen to the land. The creative impulse behind her writing, she believes, grows directly from that intimate association with earth.

Harjo's story depicts the importance of sensory contact in fostering an adaptation to the land. Soil is not only touched and smelled; it is heard. The range of sensory experience that children enjoy extends far beyond that of most adults, whose perceptions are often dulled by internal preoccupations and familiar routines. By engaging more of their senses in each moment, children can literally incorporate their discoveries, holding them as kinesthetic memories rather than cognitive recollections. Bodily imprinting may account for the sustained intensity of early memories. "The great bequest of childhood," educator Louise Chawla suggests, "is that it is a period of fresh, passionate response . . . [during which] a child absorbs sensations that give life to the growing imagination and help sustain it in maturity."[12] If ecological writers are any indication, children whose sensory channels are fully opened through explorations outdoors *do* experience heightened creativity in later life. Many writers credit their youthful attunement to the natural world with igniting their imaginations and their passion for Earth.

The gift for wholehearted concentration that children commonly have must be consciously fostered by adults. Reflecting on their own youth and being around children may help individuals relearn the art of attentiveness. Scott Momaday observes that by spending time with children we can help recall the acuity of early perspectives: among children, we "stop and catch our breath and understand that those ways of seeing the world are still very good."[13]

Children not only pay close attention to their surroundings but also meet other beings with infectious joy and disarming trust. The exuberant spirit of their early explorations may provoke a certain nostalgia in later years, when such intense immersion in the moment can be harder to achieve. Writer Zora Neale Hurston reflects: "I was only happy in the woods, and when the ecstatic Florida springtime came strolling from the sea, trance-glorifying the world with its aura . . . [I] listened to the wind soughing and sighing through the crowns of the lofty pines. I made particular friendship with one huge tree and always played about its roots. I named it 'the loving pine.'"[14]

Friends and mentors in youth are rarely confined to the human species; they may be found in the "person" of a tree, animal, rock, cave, or creek. By befriending a being that is not human, a child can extend her capacity for ecological connection. She enters into what philosopher Martin Buber terms a relation of reciprocity, where the other is not met as an object but as a fellow being (a theme developed in chapter 5). Buber suggests that a capacity to treat the other as "Thou," rather than "It," is essential to sustaining just and moral relations.

A deep feeling for other beings, more than duty or principle, may be what fosters moral responsibility. "We can be ethical," conservationist Aldo Leopold observed, "only in relation to what we can see, feel, understand, love or otherwise have faith in."[15] Certainly among ecological writers, commitment to responsible action appears to grow from emotional, sensory, and imaginative bonds to Earth forged early in life.

Childhood experiences of ecological kinship can become "touchstone memories" that reinforce moral sensibilities in adulthood.[16] Writers commonly view these memories not as ideals to recapture but as the foundation of their ecological practice. Writing of the forest she knew in childhood, novelist Barbara Kingsolver claims that "much of what I know about life, and almost everything I believe about the way I want to live, was formed in those woods."[17] Her childhood attachment to place defines her moral and spiritual views, indeed her life philosophy. That guiding vision appears to come directly from the land, not from family or school (as is commonly assumed). Kingsolver's conviction that place shapes her values and conscience reveals a spiritual humility toward the land that is notably absent in the larger culture. The woods of her childhood home, she suggests, hold a depth of wonder and wisdom that human knowledge cannot match.

Individuals appear most apt to acquire this spiritual humility when raised in unforgiving natural settings. The intense elemental forces that sculpt such habitats can awaken a healthy respect for powers that cannot be fully measured or known. Reflecting on his youth in the wooded Appalachian foothills, Edward Abbey writes: "that sultry massed deepness of transpiring green, formed the theatre of our play. . . . [T]he forest—in which it was possible to get authentically lost—sustained our sense of awe and terror in ways that fantasy cannot."[18] Having grown to love the humbling unpredictability of wild settings, Abbey sought them throughout adulthood.

Not all the memories of childhood explorations outdoors are ones of sensory delight. Terry Tempest Williams recounts her early visits to Great Salt Lake: "The ritual was always the same. Run into the lake, scream, and run back out. The salt seeped into the sores of our scraped knees and lingered. And if the stinging sensation didn't bring you to tears, the brine flies did."[19] Surprisingly, though, confrontations with nature's humbling and discomforting dimensions do not seem to detract from the intensity of children's attachments. Scott Russell Sanders, who received a snakebite at age three—losing consciousness and suffering for days from a swollen leg—reports that the experience "didn't make me wary of playing outdoors, didn't make me fearful of animals, didn't even spook me about snakes."[20]

Converts who face these challenges early in life come to respect the unruly sides of outer ecology. Few of them appear to experience crises within the natural realm, and those who do downplay their severity. In this regard, they demonstrate an unusual acceptance of ecological cycles, a sense of security that encompasses natural fluctuations. Among numerous autobiographical accounts, I found only one writer who admits that fear overshadows her experiences outdoors. She confesses wryly: "How I envy those robust, cheerful Muir-like ones who are always comfortable and uplifted in the wild! For me, it can be harrowing, and always sobering."[21] Clearly not every ecological writer finds the natural world soothing, but most do cultivate a trust in its patterns and cycles.

What can jeopardize that faith is the degradation or loss of a cherished place. Several writers attest to deep scars left by severance of their childhood links to the land. Scott Russell Sanders describes the emotional aftermath of his family's relocation from a farm in Tennessee to a military reservation in Ohio: "The move from South to North, from red dirt to concrete, from fields planted in cotton to fields planted in bombs, opened a fissure in me that I have tried to bridge, time and again, with words."[22] When a child's continuity with place is shattered, even imagination cannot fully restore the loss. Sanders seeks to mend the broken link through creative writing, but it remains a fissure in his soul.

The horror of living amidst munitions bunkers on a military arsenal left Sanders with an enduring conviction that "we build our lives in mine fields."[23] The sense of impending annihilation he experienced in that setting grew more acute as he came to recognize the global extent of ecological destruction. Sanders now fears that the future of the species may recapitulate his own past, with the whole world becoming a poisoned reservation.

Other writers witness the decimation of places that once nourished their imaginations. The woods where Abbey played as a child were subsequently clear-cut and the underlying mountain strip-mined. The outer desecration, he found, mirrored a profound inner desiccation: "Something like a shadow has fallen between present and past, an abyss wide as war that cannot be bridged . . . memory is undermined and the image of our beginnings betrayed, dissolved, rendered not mythical but illusory. We have connived in the murder of our own origins."[24] By destroying these formative places, Abbey suggests, we vandalize our very souls. He and Sanders employ similar metaphors of chasms that cannot be bridged to portray their irreparable sense of separation. Since the places that were part of them have been destroyed, they can never be whole again.

Their stories confirm the vital need to sustain "overgrown" places where our spirits and imaginations can roam. These open spaces are increasingly vulnerable as communities become more densely developed—with houses built out to lot lines and every "vacant" parcel converted to a house site or a manicured, chemically treated "recreational facility." There are fewer neighborhood "commons" where children can gather for outdoor play. Recognizing the vital importance of these local wilds in fostering a turn to Earth may give new impetus to the community land conservation movement. It is clear from the accounts of ecological writers that "the first essential adaptation" to the land has lasting repercussions throughout life. The loves and losses experienced in that time of youthful imprinting lay the foundation for a committed ecological practice.

Strong Green Cords

The childhood bond to land can be seen as an umbilical cord that joins one to the nurturing Earth, providing physical, emotional, and spiritual sustenance. The birth cord that ties a child to place may run through a parent or other relative who is deeply attached to the Earth. Alice Walker describes how love for her mother strengthened her own attachment to place: "There was a strong green cord connecting me to this great, simple seeming, but complicated woman who was herself rooted in the earth."[25] Walker's parents raised their family on rich Georgia soil, cultivating love for the land through work in their large subsistence garden. Walker characterizes her family as pagan in the oldest sense, living as country dwellers spiritually allied to Earth. Her parents' attachment to the land came to shape Walker's abiding appreciation of place.

Many ecological writers acknowledge how relatives helped guide their turn to Earth. Mentors shared in their explorations, fed their hunger for knowledge, nourished their passions, and inspired them by example. Scott Russell Sanders recounts how his father would routinely dash outdoors at the call of geese and would carry his infant son out to watch thunderstorms from the front porch. "I learned from my parents a thousand natural facts," Sanders reflects, "but above all I learned how to stand on the earth, how to address the creation, and how to listen."[26] The most essential lesson he gained was not a skill but an art: an attentive and spiritual mode of relation. From their lived example, Sanders developed the rudiments of an ecological practice. The quality of attention and reverence toward the natural world that his parents modeled became the standard shaping his own sensibility.

Sanders also found a role model in his high school science teacher, Fay Givens, a woman whose wonder in the natural world was so intense that she literally trembled when she spoke of it. Givens's devotion to plants made her subject to ridicule, but Sanders found her passion inspiring. He came to share her conviction that the miraculous abides in the common: "She taught me that if we could only be adequate to the given world, we need not dream of paradise."[27] From Givens and his parents, Sanders learned that reverence toward the world is not an option but an obligation. The beauty and mystery of the world call forth a response: to refuse that call, Sanders came to believe, is to commit the spiritual sin of acedia.

Scott Momaday received similar encouragement from mentors to acknowledge the wonderment of being. He learned from the example of relatives like his Kiowa grandmother, Aho, who embodied "a reverence for the sun, a holy regard that now is all but gone out of [hu]mankind . . . an ancient awe."[28] Her mode of living reflected a long tribal heritage that bound Kiowa Indians to the cycles of nature. That ancient awe continues to inform Momaday's own ecological practice.

Alice Walker draws inspiration from African ancestors whose tribal traditions held them close to the land. She reports that some ancestors even visit her in dreams, encouraging her quest to rekindle a spirituality bound to Earth. Although few ecological writers share such rich tribal legacies, many do find mentors who nurture their capacity for awe.

The infectious zest that mentors display for natural mysteries may move children more deeply than demonstrations of technical knowledge. Despite her scientific training, Rachel Carson downplayed the need for mentors to provide answers or explanations: "I sincerely believe that for the child, and for the parent seeking to guide him, it is not half so important to know as to feel." Feeling calls for a heightened mode of receptivity, "opening up to the disused channels of sensory impression."[29] Carson's most devoted mentor, her mother, modeled this acute receptivity and passion despite having little scientific expertise. The technical knowledge that Carson acquired came from books and formal schooling: what her mother offered was less tangible but more real. "More than anyone else I know," Carson wrote after a lifetime living alongside her mother, "she embodied Albert Schweitzer's 'reverence for life.'"[30] This philosophy recognizes the kinship of all creatures and the moral need for humans to support the well-being of other animals and plants.

Reverence might seem to be a passive stance of silent and humble appreciation, yet it can spark a commitment to assertive action. Rachel Carson notes that while her mother was "gentle and compassionate, she could fight fiercely against anything she believed wrong."[31] That paradoxical mix of fierce compassion became a potent force in Carson's own life, particularly in her protracted campaign against the misuse of pesticides.

Terry Tempest Williams learned fierce compassion from her grandmother Mimi, an avowed activist long before the birth of the environmental movement. Through Mimi's support and example, Williams grew to face "life directly, to not be afraid of risking oneself for fear of losing too much."[32] Edward Abbey gained a similar inner strength through the bond with his father, a practicing socialist. Abbey absorbed some of his father's philosophical views and all his faith in a life of active resistance. In the dedication to his book *The Journey Home*, Abbey credits his father with teaching him "to hate injustice, to defy the powerful, and to speak for the voiceless." Abbey maintained this family legacy through his iconoclastic writing and his monkey-wrenching (nonviolent sabotage that he performed in defense of Earth).

The most influential mentors are often family members or friends, but ecological writers also find models of compassionate resistance in works of environmental literature. Contact with literary mentors can reinforce and extend the influence of relatives.

The Alchemy of Words

Stories read in childhood have broadened the vision and affirmed the aspirations of many ecological converts. Some writers gained an early appreciation for the natural world through animal tales by authors such as Ernest Thompson Seton, Thornton Burgess, and Jack London. Terry Tempest Williams's family, for example, would return to cherished animal stories each winter, reading them aloud.

Books can ignite the imagination, transporting a child to realms beyond everyday existence and awakening lifelong passions. Rachel Carson spent time in her early years exploring the woods and streams of her family's sixty-five-acre tract in western Pennsylvania, but her focus came to rest on a habitat she knew only through reading. Carson recalls how "as a very small child I was fascinated by the ocean, although I had never seen it. I dreamed of it and longed to see it, and I read all the sea literature I could find."[33] She did not visit the sea until after college, but it was part of her inner ecology from early childhood. Her enduring fascination with the ocean ultimately led Carson to write three books exploring its mysteries.

Terry Tempest Williams recalls experiencing a similar draw to unknown realms in childhood. For her, the lure lay not in water but in air. When her grandmother gave her Peterson's *Field Guide to Western Birds*, Williams poured over it endlessly, "dreaming about the birds, imagining the birds long before I ever saw them." They became "an extension of family," she explains, mentors from the "more-than-human world."[34]

Books can serve as wise elders, sharing the culture's accumulated wisdom and helping both children and adults interpret their experiences outdoors.[35] Scott Russell Sanders refers to the restorative and transformative power of words as the "alchemy" of reading, where marks on a page transmute into vital and sustaining narratives.[36] Even children raised in storytelling traditions may find that books enrich their ecological learning. Scott Momaday, Alice Walker, and Terry Tempest Williams grew up in cultures that valued storytelling, yet they all discovered literary elders who helped extend their vision and give voice to values held deep within.

The power of ecological books may rest as much in the character of the authors as in the literary merits of their works. Many classics of ecological literature—Thoreau's *Walden*, Leopold's *A Sand County Almanac*, Carson's *Silent Spring*, and Beston's *The Outermost House*—reflect principles that grounded the authors' lives. Such writers are not only gifted artists but ethical exemplars. Edward Abbey and Scott Russell Sanders both observe that they have been touched most deeply by authors who demonstrate moral vision, courage, and a recognition of the larger whole. Terry Tempest Williams, who began reading works by ecological writers during adolescence, found in their lived examples a template for her own path. She draws continual inspiration from these spiritual pioneers: "We can never forget the power of impassioned, informed voices telling their story, bearing witness, speaking out on behalf of the land."[37]

Through literary mentors, ecological writers gain courage to find their own voices and articulate their convictions: "not until I began to read the literature of natural history," reflects writer Stephen Trimble, "could I articulate my belief in the Earth as grounding and faith and guide."[38] The solidarity lent by literary mentors appears particularly important for writers who grow up with views that differ markedly from the perspectives of family and friends. Williams, for example, found little support for her ecological convictions among peers who adhered to Mormon conventions. The "impassioned, informed voices" of literary mentors, therefore, helped lend her courage to challenge the status quo and pursue her turn to Earth.

Re-turning

For many individuals, the wellspring of ecological conversion rests in childhood. The imaginative fusion with place that occurs in early years allows the land to imprint deeply on their psyches and souls. Most children experience the natural world as both real and imaginary, a landscape that simultaneously embodies the actual and the possible. This perspective awakens a sense of wonder and dissolves some of the established boundaries that separate humans from the rest of nature. By forming friends across species lines, children extend their capacity for relation. This youthful impulse can evolve by adulthood into a steadfast compassion for other beings and a commitment to "speak for the voiceless."

Early roots of environmental commitment are evident among educators and activists, as well as ecological writers. Surveys of environmental educators confirm the importance both of their childhood experiences outdoors and their influential mentors. Scholar David Orr suggests that "virtually all environmental activists . . . were shaped early on by relation to a specific place." That childhood bond, he writes, "exerts a magical effect on the ecological imagination. And without such experiences, few have ever become ardent and articulate defenders of nature."[39]

Recalling our early devotion to the land can strengthen our trust in natural cycles and our sense of belonging to a larger whole. In this way, remembrance becomes a religious act in the oldest, etymological sense (*re-ligare,* meaning to bind together), rejoining lost and neglected dimensions of the self. Through acts of remembrance, we can uncover the roots of our ecological practice. Significant experiences with the land in childhood may be essential prerequisites to any subsequent turn to Earth: "those ties with the earth and the farm animals and growing things," writer Willa Cather once observed, "are never made at all unless they are made early."[40] Ties made early, these writers demonstrate, can hold throughout life.

One Reader's Remembrance

As far back as memory extends, my identity is intertwined with a sea-rimmed world of stone, sand, and spruce. Our family lived for part of each summer in this place of paradox. What looks like an island is really a mountaintop whose surrounding valleys flooded after the last glacial recession. With soil not sufficient to hide the rock, this ancient hill supports a thriving array of species. The stony shores, born of a volcano, carry scars from glacial ice. The island's woods, meadows, and beaches hold a sense of timeless familiarity and endless mystery.

My senses first came alive on this improbable isle, instinctively absorbing images and lessons from its elemental life. The cascading cycles of tides and weather dictated the course of each day. We rose and retired with the sun, set our travel plans by the tide, and lived a life of rich simplicity—dwelling in a cabin built from island spruce, heating with wood, and bathing in rainwater.

Ours was the only human family on the island, so our sense of community embraced other species. Our immediate neighbors included resident crows, gulls, voles, and a steady stream of migratory warblers. Just offshore, eider chicks hardly larger than dandelion puffs would surf white-capped waters. The harbor seals were our most charismatic neighbors, but I was equally attached to more homely creatures such as barnacles and sow bugs. One June, my brother David and I made daily visits to a hive of yellow jackets lodged among tree roots, bearing plates laden with honey and marshmallows.

As children we had great latitude to explore the island—creating games and rituals, making forts and rafts, scrambling through rockweed and wading into pungent blue-black mudflats. Icy waters, strong currents, steep cliffs, and sharp rocks made the setting treacherous. Yet our parents did not confine us. They cautioned us of these dangers, and with their gentle guidance, the place taught us well.

For several summers we holed up in a driftwood spaceship that we named, oblivious to its redundancy, "Karl Street Road." The ramshackle collection of sun-bleached boards, which drew structural strength from a rock cliff, faced south, and the surrounding beach could get uncomfortably hot during midday hours. Then the spaceship offered a cool, dark haven from which to survey the squintingly bright world, as we hunched like animals in our lair.

Our parents introduced us to the rituals of place—watching the sun's descent behind a neighboring island, stirring the waters for signs of phosphorescence, and finding constellations in the night sky. Even in routine tasks such as gathering firewood or hauling water, we found the place continually reawakening us. A walk to the compost pile might reveal a monarch butterfly perched on goldenrod. The routine motion of sawing firewood could be interrupted by a loon's plaintive call.

The remembrance of those moments, held through the winter, was renewed and deepened each June. Our island life in Maine held an intensity that suburban existence could not match. Late in high school, I wrote an essay declaring my allegiance to Maine, stating (in the unequivocal tone of an adolescent) that while my mailing address and driver's license identified me as a resident of Maryland, I considered Maine home. My attachment to the island spawned an interest in environmental issues that was evident by middle school and has directed my studies and work ever since.

My educational path turned out to be long and circuitous: through two-plus decades of formal schooling, I attended more than a dozen different institutions and programs. My migratory movements came in part from seeking something that did not yet exist. The field of environmental studies was just coming of age during my high school and college years, and little had yet been written on environmental ethics, philosophy, or ecocriticism.

Through this extended quest, my parents stood behind me—affirming their belief in my abilities and the value of my unconventional vision. They both had walked untrammeled paths, personally and professionally, and believed that their children should follow their passions (knowing, from experience, that such a course rarely led to fame or fortune). Their mentoring came through lived example. My father pursued independent work that inspired him, declining the academic and bureaucratic positions that would have provided security at too great a price. My mother sustained her elemental connections to the Earth by creating and enjoying a natural oasis for wildlife in the midst of suburbia. Together they modeled lives of enduring passions and values.

My parents took pride in quietly subverting the typical consumer lifestyle. In the course of four decades, they have owned only three cars. They ran errands and commuted to work by foot, bicycle, and public transit. On a street of manicured, chemically treated lawns, their front yard was a veritable jungle of forsythia, azalea, transplanted Maine spruce trees, and perennial flowers.

Growing up on the margins of suburban culture made it easier for me to adopt and sustain values outside the mainstream. I acquired from my parents the habits of questioning reflexive consumption and of judging actions by their broader environmental impacts. That impulse strengthened during adolescence, as I began discovering the testimony of writers with a strong ecological conscience. The works of John Muir, E. B. White, Wendell Berry, and other ecological writers became the focus of my college honors project, compiling and editing an anthology of poems and prose depicting perspectives on ecological degradation and healing. That engaging experience launched me into a life of ecological writing— along the coast of Maine, of course.

3

Reflection

I think all human beings have to go through this because
eventually, inevitably we are alone and there is that peace
no one can give you, really, other than coming to grips
with and confronting your own life and your own destiny,
what work you have done and what work you need to do.

—Denise Chavez in Balassi, Crawford, and Eysturoy,
This Is about Vision

Seeds of an ecological practice sown in childhood can be nourished
in later years by periods of intensive introspection. During these
times, individuals reassess their calling in life and their place within
the natural whole. The contours of inner ecology change as old
assumptions erode, familiar bearings disappear, and new convictions
take root.

This inner flux can prove challenging: one must live for a time
without the security of the known or a clear vision for the future.
The temporal chasm between old and new constitutes what Terry
Tempest Williams terms the "deep trench" of reflection.[1] Entering
this trench represents a metaphoric descent into Earth, a journey to
elemental depths. One's scope of vision is constricted, forcing the
mind inward. Time in the trench can be a test of faith, calling one

to "trust in the darkness, trust in the invisible; [that] is the act of courage which the convert must summon up from the deepest part of his being."[2]

Those who enter the trench encounter polarities that cannot be reconciled: the pull of stability and push of change; the necessity of death to nourish life; and the simultaneous draw of solitude and community. This dynamic balance of contradictory forces can generate a creative tension that is unsettling but ultimately valuable. The paradoxes help converts adopt a more fluid and cyclical outlook on life and begin feeling their turns to Earth.

Reflection affords an opportunity to regain energy and perspective. Scholar James Loder defines it as an "interlude for scanning" in which one searches for solutions, not actively or aggressively, but attentively—waiting, wondering, and following hunches.[3] Navigating the trench of reflection can prompt one to reassess what matters most and commit to living with greater ecological integrity.

When Hope Recedes

Reflection can occur deliberately or unwittingly, or it can come about through a combination of choice and chance. Some individuals consciously invite reflection by dwelling in places where natural patterns predominate and they can attend to the continual resonance between outer and inner ecology. For others, reflective periods are neither anticipated nor welcomed. Individuals may descend into the trench due to a debilitating illness or the loss of a cherished place or friend. Introspection can also be sparked by a pervasive sense of estrangement from the broader culture and by efforts to challenge the pervasive cultural apathy that exacerbates ecological degradation.

Rampant destruction of natural systems appears, in converts' eyes, to defy both heart and reason, countering ethical and religious injunctions to honor creation and our instinctual desire for self-preservation. Our society's seeming incapacity to address ecological problems may stem from acute denial, a mental paralysis known to psychologists as "psychic numbing." When faced with the potential of vast devastation, our minds tend to shut down or compartmentalize to avoid total breakdown.[4] One can comprehend the death of an individual animal or the loss of an ecosystem, but the mind ceases to process information in a meaningful way when confronted with the extinction of countless species. Psychic numbing can block an appropriate response to threats and so exacerbate the current crises.

Ecological converts strive to awaken from this societal stupor by questioning familiar "truths" and assumptions. In seeking to confront the implications of the atomic age, Rachel Carson discovered how hard this process can be:

> Some of the thoughts that came were so unattractive to me that I rejected them completely, for the old ideas die hard, especially when they are emotionally as well as intellectually dear to one. It was pleasant to believe, for example, that much of Nature was forever beyond the tampering reach of man. . . .
>
> These beliefs have almost been part of me for as long as I have thought about such things. To have them even vaguely threatened was so shocking that, as I have said, I shut my mind—refused to acknowledge what I couldn't help seeing.[5]

Carson's experience illustrates the challenge of facing up to the full magnitude of environmental loss.

Denial can give way to an overwhelming sense of defeat. Despair represents a different, but no less potent, form of psychological paralysis. It may arise in response to the chasm that stretches between the inviting possibility of an ideal society and the stark reality of the status quo. Those who hold high ideals for themselves and their communities can feel this discrepancy acutely.

A devastating sense of living in a broken world struck Kentucky writer Wendell Berry, for example, when he visited the mining country near his home and witnessed poverty, alienation, social deprivation, and ecological devastation on a scale unprecedented in his experience. He returned home in a state of existential defeat, filled with "a most oppressive and persistent sense of the smallness of human hopes before the inertia of institutions and machines."[6] The sheer force and magnitude of industrial destruction pulverized his visions for social and ecological harmony. Berry eventually overcame this paralyzing despair by reflecting on the experience, writing his way from hopelessness into renewed moral resolve.

Despair can also stem from a personal failure to realize ecological and ethical ideals. Converts who fail to embody their highest values risk feeding the corrosive habits of the broader society. Edward Abbey, for example, admits: "I live falsely. I do not practice what I preach. I wanted a life of freedom, passion, simplicity; I lead instead a life of complicated deals, petty routines, rancorous internal grievances, moral compromise, sloth, acedia, and vanity."[7]

Failure to realize personal ideals can make it harder to believe that the larger culture will ever extricate itself from moral and ecological quagmire. Yet such failures are inevitable, given the fallibility of human nature and the exigencies of contemporary society. Modern living, Scott Russell Sanders observes, affords no moral purity: "The choice is not between innocence and guilt, the choice is between more and less complicity."[8] Routine compromise of one's ecological ideals can erode hope for meaningful change, leaving the dubious consolation of small victories and resounding defeats. Rachel Carson voiced her exasperation at this debilitating pattern: "Life is such a queer business—great visions, great opportunities opened up, and then a door slammed. I don't understand it; I never will."[9] Repeated individual and collective setbacks can erode one's faith in the possibility for meaningful ecological change.

Few writers escape the broad reach of disappointment, doubt, and despair, but many weather the darkness without losing sight of their ideals. Times of reflection seem to help them regain inner equilibrium. Edward Abbey attests to his success navigating through bleak spells: "The despair that haunts the background of our lives, sometimes obtruding itself into consciousness, can still be modulated, as I know from experience, into a comfortable melancholia and from there to defiance, delight, a roaring affirmation of self-existence.

Even, at times, into a quiet and blessedly self-forgetful peace, a modest joy."[10] As despair ebbs, an abiding sense of vitality and gratitude may return, a remembrance that one is graced with existence in a less than perfect world.

Periods of reflection can temper unbridled idealism, initiating a sobering but essential period of growth. By freeing one from the hold of unconsidered assumptions, reflexive responses, and preconditioned patterns, time in the trench can transform grand visions into humble plans. Those who are intent upon preserving pristine wilderness and living with ecological purity may come to acknowledge that there are no untrammeled places and no flawless means of ecological practice. The acute anguish and remorse provoked by ecological destruction may be assuaged by recognizing that the natural whole will endure, even if diminished. Converts humbled by experiences in the trench often find renewed energy to undertake what work they need to do.

Sojourns Outdoors

The humility experienced in reflective periods may be reinforced through time spent in untamed nature. Ecological converts commonly make sojourns outdoors to awaken themselves to unrealized dimensions of being. Nature holds great power to evoke inner transformation, according to both religious scholars and ecological writers. Studies of traditional religious converts reveal that "natural beauty" is among the most common antecedents of a transformative spiritual experience.[11] Centuries of nature writing confirm the power of outdoor experiences to foster a sense of mystical interconnection with the whole (a theme developed in chapter 4).

Opportunities for reflection may be greatest when forays outdoors are undertaken alone, with attention wholly focused on the experience of place. A craving for solitude, commonly judged as misanthropic, can be a means of deepening relations across species lines. Scott Russell Sanders writes that his hunger to interact with other species reflects not a "distaste for humanity, but . . . a need to experience my humanness the more vividly by confronting stretches of the earth that my kind has had no part in making."[12] Stepping outside human communities may prompt a deeper appreciation for the mystery of existence.

Interludes in natural settings, often characterized as "retreats" from civilization, are more aptly a meeting with—and merging into—nature. Some of the best-known texts in environmental literature chronicle extended times of solitude outdoors: such as Henry David Thoreau's *Walden,* Annie Dillard's *Pilgrim at Tinker Creek,* Henry Beston's *The Outermost House,* Gretel Ehrlich's *The Solace of Open Spaces,* and Edward Abbey's *Desert Solitaire.* In their sojourns outdoors, these writers do not aim for religious reclusion—withdrawing from the material world to worship a transcendent deity. They seek to immerse themselves in the larger whole, blurring the lines between self and world. Thoreau writes that his goal in living at Walden Pond is to face life deliberately, to participate fully in the experience of being: "I wanted to live deep and suck out all the marrow of life," he asserts, regardless of whether it proved "mean" or "sublime."[13]

Engagement in the broader ecological community can transform identity, moving one from a relation of detached objectivity to one of intimate kinship. The ideal Thoreau sought was a felt sense of participation: "I to be nature looking into nature."[14] Terry Tempest Williams seems to approach this ideal at times during solo visits to a bird refuge. Apart from other humans, she is able to sense the patterns of life about her. The solitude, she writes, "sustains me and protects me from my mind. It renders me fully present. . . . There are other languages being spoken by wind, water, and wings. There are other lives to consider."[15] The quiet of solitary reflection allows Williams to find her place within the larger web of being.

A participatory sense of relation can dissolve the hierarchical divisions that traditionally separate species. Other beings, once seen as objects, become subjects in their own right—what Henry Beston termed "other nations, caught with ourselves in the net of life and time, fellow prisoners of the splendour and travail of the earth."[16]

When one participates fully in the natural world, a utilitarian view that objectifies the other can give way to a reverent appreciation for that being's intrinsic value. In this way, immersion in the broader natural community may evoke an ethic of kinship.

Edward Abbey found that close contact with other species irrevocably changed his worldview. Walking daily through the tranquil depth of an aspen grove prompted Abbey to wonder about "those beings, alive, sentient, transpiring" that surrounded him. In the company of trees, he came to conclude, one meets beings with a "conscious presence."[17] This realization challenged his empirical and analytical training and affirmed his abiding affinity for trees. Countless other writers attest to how the vivid immediacy of elemental life, when given full focus, confirms a sense of belonging in an animate world—a conviction that often traces back to childhood.

Alongside restorative outdoor experiences are some that induce fear. Nature's steady patterns can give way to unforeseen crises, forcing individuals to reassess their fundamental relation to the ecological whole. In *Refuge,* Terry Tempest Williams chronicles the rise of Great Salt Lake as it flooded a migratory bird refuge that had become her spiritual sanctuary. The ecological damage without comes to mirror psychic losses within. Distinctions between her outer and inner landscape dissolve as Williams struggles to find some solid ground. The only refuge, she comes to realize, lies in embracing change—in moving with the swelling, swirling waters. Facing the wilds without helps Williams recognize the need to honor the wilds within.

Encounters with nature's destructive sides can test the commitment of ecological converts, providing a potent reminder that a turn to Earth is not a move toward stability, security, or endless bounty. The Earth offers great constancy in its seasonal cycles and shifting population dynamics, but that constancy is not wholly free of chaos. Those who spend extensive time outdoors learn to honor nature's fierce spontaneity. Humility becomes an essential survival skill.

Living in desert country, Terry Tempest Williams has had to contend with rattlesnakes and scorpions, heat stroke, flash floods, and a hiking accident that split her head open "like a peach hitting pavement."[18] These experiences have bred a healthy respect for the desert's hazards without diminishing Williams's devotion to the natural world. Reflecting on the liabilities of an outdoor life, she suggests that the physical and emotional challenges can build character. In the presence of elemental powers, the senses grow more acute as control diminishes: "To enter wilderness is to court risk, and risk favors the senses, enabling one to live well."[19] Williams concludes that an ecological practice, because it fosters spiritual and moral bonds with other beings, necessarily entails risk. One cannot hold heart and senses open, she finds, without experiencing moments of acute loss.

Meeting Death within Life

Painful times of relinquishment can prompt individuals to reassess their life purpose and deepen their commitment to Earth. Grief shatters complacency, precluding a return to comfortable but outmoded ways of being. In the spaces held open by grief, there is room and time for new growth. Loss leads into a paradoxical realm in which one is challenged—simultaneously—to let go and receive, to die in order to live more deeply. Writer Gretel Ehrlich observes that loss "constitutes an odd kind of fullness; despair empties out into an unquenchable appetite for life."[20] As individuals reflect on the place of death within life, they often gain a greater appreciation for life's fragility and its resilience.

The transforming power of loss marks Terry Tempest Williams's book *Refuge* and the personal letters of Rachel Carson. Both women faced the death of close family members early in adulthood. By the age of thirty, Carson had lost her father and sister (and subsequently both of her sister's children died young). Williams, at thirty-four, became matriarch of her family, having lost her mother, grandmothers, and four other relatives to cancer. Forced to accept the incontrovertible presence of death within life, both writers chose to live—in Carson's words—"more affirmatively, making the most of opportunities when they are offered, not putting them off for another day."[21] Recognizing the unearned gift of their own lives sparked a commitment to live purposefully.

The repeated loss of family members may have helped strengthen Carson's capacity to face her own illness and premature death. During work on *Silent Spring,* an exposé detailing the damage wrought by synthetic chemicals, Carson was diagnosed with malignant cancer, severe arthritis, iritis, and a host of other ailments. Her subject matter gained a poignant immediacy as she realized that her own disease could stem from exposure to toxic compounds. Part of Carson's determination to complete *Silent Spring* despite crippling medical conditions grew from her hope that this work might spare others a similar fate: "Knowing the facts as I did," she wrote, "I could not rest until I had brought them to public attention."[22] Carson found she could face death only by doing her utmost to sustain the greater whole of life.

Death's imminence reinforced, rather than diminished, Carson's abiding sense of life's essential beauty and integrity. Reflecting on the "closing journey" of migrating monarch butterflies and on her own approaching demise, Carson wrote to a friend: "when that intangible cycle has run its course it is a natural and not unhappy thing that a life comes to its end. That is what those brightly fluttering bits of life taught me this morning. I found a deep happiness in it—so, I hope, may you."[23] Making peace with the life-death cycle helped deepen Carson's spiritual love for the world and her commitment to action. She worked persistently in her final years to share her ecological insights. One of her greatest griefs in dying young, she noted, was to leave with so much writing still in her.

Few individuals face the severe trials that Carson did, but many encounter periods of loss or illness that induce reflection. A confrontation with "pain, failure, suffering and inevitable nonbeing," scholar Paul Brockelman suggests, is an essential prerequisite to spiritual transformation.[24] It can challenge one's foundational beliefs, providing a test of faith. Those who place their trust in natural cycles may find that a prolonged experience of illness or loss can prove spiritually as well as physically debilitating.

Through three years of acute suffering from Lyme disease, Alice Walker struggled to make sense of her experience. She felt betrayed by nature and fearful of spending time outdoors since she had contracted the disease from a tick and could get reinfected. Yet in the midst of doubt and despair, she still drew sustenance from "the sight of trees, the scent of the ocean, the feel of the wind and the warmth of the sun," all of which remained "faithful" to her.[25] Walker's dilemma constitutes a classic crisis of faith in which she simultaneously doubts and depends on her primary spiritual source. She cannot rely on the beneficence of nature (as one might an omnipotent God), but she still takes sensual and spiritual comfort in its presence.

As her body weakened, Walker found that her spirit grew stronger: it was "as if my illness had pushed open an inner door that my usual consciousness was willing to ignore."[26] Walker came to view her disease as a protracted invitation to reaffirm her faith in and love for the natural world. It acted as a spiritual rite of passage, reminding her to attend to connections and practice relinquishment. Loss— whether of health, work, friends, or dreams—can dispel the illusion that we are the sole shapers of our destinies. Dropped unceremoniously into humility, we are forced to acknowledge that we dwell amid mystery.

Walker's experience demonstrates the power of what one psychiatrist terms "positive disintegration," a challenging phase of relinquishment that precedes reconstruction of belief and identity.[27] Not all losses or tragedies are redeemed in this way, but many of those recorded by ecological writers ultimately do have some positive outcome (leaving open to question whether there are experiences of unredeemed disintegration that go unrecorded).

Dwelling on the Margins

Although not every loss is turned to advantage, many writers find that the seeming handicap of being marginalized by mainstream culture actually fosters their ecological awakenings. Maintaining a critical distance from prevailing beliefs allows individuals to reflect critically on cultural patterns and practices. Freed from reflexive participation in societal norms and customary expectations regarding family, household, and religion, they can pursue lifestyles that favor creativity over convention.

Rachel Carson, Terry Tempest Williams, and Alice Walker, for example, all chose family patterns outside the norm, seeking more opportunities for creative reflection than motherhood in a conventional nuclear family commonly affords. Carson spent her adult life in a matrifocal household that comprised her mother, herself, and—at various times—her nieces and grandnephew. As the primary breadwinner, Carson could delegate many domestic chores and devote more time to writing. Williams, like Carson, has close bonds with three generations of her family. Yet she and her husband, Brooke, have chosen not to become parents, giving her more time and creative energy for writing. Walker valued growing up in a large family but has found that she treasures the freedom of a more solitary life. After raising her daughter (as the primary single parent), Walker has balanced times of partnership with generous doses of solitude. All three women configured their lives in ways to nourish their art.

Other writers part with societal norms by valuing attachment to place over career advancement. Scott Russell Sanders, for example, moved from native soil early in his career to follow promising academic opportunities. He met with professional success but felt displaced—deprived of some essential nourishment that only a familiar landscape could provide. As he acknowledged this sense of loss, his loyalty shifted. He chose to return to home terrain, taking a less prestigious position to be in a place he loved. "I cannot have a spiritual center," Sanders writes, "without having a geographical one; I cannot live a grounded life without being grounded in a place."[28]

Sanders's strong faith in his convictions comes in part from living outside mainstream social circles (beginning in college—where he was a poor midwesterner among affluent easterners). Watching and listening on the margins, he believes, has sharpened his powers of discernment: "I was free to envision a way of life more desirable and durable than this one that excluded me."[29] Sanders credits his peripheral social status with strengthening his ecological practice: digging beneath surface appearances has helped him ground his life on a core connection to Earth and family.

Alice Walker believes that her "position as an outcast" growing up (due to her race and a childhood accident that blinded her in one eye) lent her the capacity to "really see people and things, to really notice relationships."[30] This ability to recognize interconnections may have nourished her compassion and moral concern for others. Walker suggests that in ways both metaphoric and literal she has one eye focused on the world about her and one eye focused on the world within. This dual vision helps her honor both outer and inner ecology.

Dwelling on the periphery can prompt one to reassess prevailing cultural beliefs, questioning the entrenched divide that separates humans from other animals. Ecological writers strive to bridge this long-standing schism by acting as shamans, venturing into new spiritual and intellectual terrain and carrying back stories and insights to their communities. This demanding role requires one to learn "what it means to be dismembered and brought to wholeness again and . . . [to face] the powerful realities, both positive and destructive, of the spiritual world."[31] Rachel Carson experienced the process of writing *Silent Spring* as a kind of shamanic journey in which she reported entering a realm so alien that she felt lonely and even a little afraid. In the face of fears and setbacks, her commitment to heal the larger community sustained her courage.

Alongside its tensions and ambiguities, a marginal existence affords critical insights into the dominant culture. For this reason, many ecological writers prefer to dwell on the periphery: "I am— really am—an extremist," Edward Abbey observed, "one who lives and loves by choice far out on the very verge of things. . . . That's the way I like it."[32] Few ecological writers are as extreme or anarchistic as Abbey, but many find that they can best live out their ecological values from a vantage point "on the very verge of things."

A few converts, though, find the marginal life overshadowed by a sense of estrangement. This pattern surfaces particularly among Native Americans and other minorities who experience a "destructive dissonance" from dwelling simultaneously within two irreconcilable cultures.[33] Norms and values of tribal life or of a particular subculture can contradict the dictates of Western industrial society, creating an untenable bind for those who live in both realms. Scott Momaday has found that he can mitigate the dissonance of living in disparate cultures by reflecting on his mixed ancestry: "My father being a Kiowa and my mother being mostly European, I guess I had a sense of living in those two areas as a child and it became important to me to understand as clearly as I could who I was and what my cultural resources were."[34] Drawing on his ancestral tradition for guiding life narratives has helped Momaday shape a more durable ecological practice.

Surfacing

Creative arts can help converts express insights that arise during reflective periods. By faithfully recording mundane events and ideas over time, ecological writers compile a narrative collage of their time in the trench. As their stories accumulate, patterns take form. Detailed journals that Terry Tempest Williams kept through four years of poignant and protracted loss became the basis for her book *Refuge*, a reflection on the spiritual necessity of making peace with change. Writing helped Williams navigate through that difficult and uncertain period, enabling her to see patterns and gain a "greater sense of trust in the process of life."[35] Ecological writers often rely on the reflective practice of writing to regain perspective and stamina when they feel discouraged or overwhelmed by personal challenges or societal problems.

Writing can even provide a vital life line, as Alice Walker testifies. She faced an unwanted pregnancy near the end of college and lay in bed for three days with a razor blade under her pillow, contemplating suicide. In preparing to leave life, she explains, "I realized how much I loved it, and how hard it would be not to see the sunrise every morning."[36] Walker had an abortion and wrote in the subsequent week almost all the poems that appeared in her first book. It was writing those poems, she reflects, that "clarified for me how very much I love being alive."[37] Writing can validate the truth of hard experience, whether the moments are crushing or healing. Walker came to rely on writing to deepen her ecological practice by fostering a dialogue between the world about her and the world within.

Many converts find that conscious introspection allows them to transmute raw feelings into a renewed resolve to value life and care for the Earth. The experience of suffering, philosopher Albert Schweitzer suggests, tempers the "soft iron of youthful idealism . . . into the steel of a full grown idealism which can never be lost."[38] Time in the trench fosters this transformation, strengthening both character and faith in the unfathomable mystery of being.

One Reader's Reflection

I stumbled into the deep trench of reflection unexpectedly, at a time when—to outward appearances—my life had just settled down after the entropic, exploratory years that followed college. Back along the coast of Maine, my heart's home, I was living along a tidal estuary where the dance of elements and creatures outside my windows kept me attuned to the pulse of the natural world. From my desk, I would watch ducks riding ice floes downriver, the crescent moon rising, and the tide sliding soundlessly in amidst spartina grasses.

My primary job at that time involved publications work for an organization engaged in land conservation. It was a professional niche I had long sought—with good colleagues, fair compensation, a flexible working schedule, and, most important, a mission that I believed in wholeheartedly.

Yet there was, as converts are wont to say, something missing. The writing I did for work often was disconnected from my spiritual and sensory experience of the land. I described places that I had never been, enumerated the economic benefits of open space, and outlined legal and financial strategies for conservation. This technical information was critical to convey, but it overlooked an essential element. Few families conserved their properties solely for financial reasons. They were motivated primarily by love for the land, a deep spiritual and emotional bond that typically went unacknowledged throughout the conservation process. The tactical dimensions of outer ecological work overshadowed the vital importance of this inner spark.

I came to see that this dynamic was not unique to land conservation. It surfaced throughout the environmental field, where political and practical pressures routinely preclude discussion of underlying spiritual and moral concerns. Almost everyone I knew (myself included) became ensnared in this trap—getting caught in a torrent of professional demands that left little time for reflection.

The longer I joined in this tacit neglect of inner ecology, though, the more discouraged I became. I felt increasingly disconnected from my own center, unable to share my core passions and sensibilities through my work. For years, writing had been a vital means by which I sensed the infinite links between inner and outer ecology. Now that element of discovery and grace was gone—taking with it much of the joy in writing.

Hoping to restore that missing vitality, I decided to trade my secure job for a course of study that held little promise of professional advancement—an interdisciplinary exploration of ecological ethics and spiritual values. Reason argued against the move, but thankfully intuition won out. Stepping back from the workaday world for a few years gave me a chance to indulge in the benefits of trench life—asking larger questions, weaving together insights from diverse fields, and discovering a larger community of individuals who sought a renewed relation to Earth.

4

Revelation

You know those moments you have when you enter a
silence that's still and complete and peaceful? That's the
source, the place where everything comes from. In that
space, you know everything is connected, that there's an
ecology of everything. In that place it is possible for people
to have a change of heart, a change of thinking, a change
in their way of being and living in the world.

—Linda Hogan in Jensen, *Listening to the Land*

In their turns to Earth, many writers experience transformative
moments when they know beyond doubt that everything is connected. They sense the tangible but invisible bonds that join all life
and elemental matter. These awakenings can foster a sense of reverence, a heartfelt conviction that spirit inheres in the world. By dis-
closing the miraculous within the ordinary, revelations hold the
power to strengthen an ecological practice and reconfigure one's life.

The power of these luminous moments is at once profound and
elusive. Revelatory insights defy the bounds of reason: their transformative power manifests in a change of heart more than in a
change of mind. Poet Rainer Maria Rilke terms them "indescribably
swift, deep, timeless moments of . . . divine inseeing."[1] Rilke's image

is akin to Emerson's famous transparent eyeball metaphor, suggesting a capacity to look simultaneously without and within: the divine sees into one even as one sees into the divine. This spiritual exchange carries one beyond ordinary perception into a timeless realm that holds unexpected dimensions of being.

Revelations can awaken awe and humility even among those who stand outside formal religion. Few ecological writers envision the divine in conventional Christian terms as a transcendent deity in human form. What holds ultimate meaning for them is not what lies *beyond* this world but the mystery embedded *within* it. Relinquishing the traditional quest for salvation and meaning in a life hereafter, they tend toward the heretical view that "the environment, nature, is the ground of a positive and sufficient joy."[2] Earth, rather than being a stepping-stone to "higher" realms, becomes the foundation of their spiritual faith and practice. Close attention to the elemental world yields ample spiritual inspiration: "Only petty minds and trivial souls yearn for supernatural events," Edward Abbey asserts, "incapable of perceiving that everything—everything!—within and around them is pure miracle."[3]

What makes the natural realm miraculous is how all the elements and beings join in a unified but dynamic whole. Some writers portray this ecological web in classical terms as the "balance of nature"; others acknowledge the presence of randomness and chaos without wholly forfeiting their intuitive sense of an intrinsic harmony. The way the world coheres is no mere accident, they insist. What holds it together and sustains it, though, is hard to define. Writer Laurens van der Post describes this abiding harmony as "the pattern that we call God."[4] His appellation captures the ecumenical view of ecological writers who envision a sacred presence immanent in nature's creative unfolding. The pattern they call God is not a static entity but rather a fluid force of growth and decay and becoming.

Like their predecessors in the Romantic tradition, ecological writers witness this dynamic divinity in the natural world, prompting varied forms of revelation—from visions and experiences of fusion with the whole to a transformed sense of self and surroundings.

Moments of acute attunement to the full breadth of being can lead one to identify others not as objects in isolation but as subjects in relation. Buddhist monk Thich Nhat Hanh describes this perspective as participatory, in that one enters into the experience of another.[5] Empathic connection can prompt a deeper sense of belonging in the world and a stronger commitment to sustain the whole (a theme developed in chapter 5, "Reciprocity").

A Truth Surpassing Reason

What sets revelatory insights apart from mundane experience is the internal conviction of their significance. "Crystalline moments," as writer Anne Morrow Lindbergh termed them, register at a level beneath reason with a certainty that brooks no dissuasion.[6] They embody paradox, being clear and convincing insights that point toward impenetrable mysteries. The exceptional clarity of a crystalline moment may be evident only to the subject involved; to others, the experience can seem vague or implausible. One of the greatest challenges writers face is finding language that fairly reflects their revelations. Religious scholar Evelyn Underhill depicts the irony of this dilemma: "there is no certitude that equals the mystics [yet] no impotence more complete than that which falls on those who try to communicate it."[7]

This dynamic is particularly pronounced in secular Western culture, which often denigrates accounts of spiritual revelation, whether they take conventional or naturalistic forms. Revelatory truths defy dominant positivist views, making it hard for those steeped in scientific rationalism to trust the wisdom of their inner senses.

Empirical training can cleave mind and heart, leaving one struggling to reconcile a reflexive skepticism with the heartfelt truth of lived experience. On a visit to his childhood home long after his father's death, Scott Russell Sanders approached trees that he and his father had planted decades earlier. Touching their bark, he began to cry and called out to his father, sensing his presence nearby. Moments later, Sanders heard a cry overhead and looked up to see a bird circling slowly above him. "It was a red-tailed hawk for sure," Sanders affirms, "and it was also my father. Not a symbol of my father, not a reminder, not a ghost, but the man himself, right there, circling in the air above me."[8]

Anticipating the reader's skepticism, and assuaging his own, Sanders continues: "The voice of my education told me then and tells me now that I did not meet my father, that I merely projected my longing onto a bird. My education may well be right; yet nothing I heard in school, nothing I've read, no lesson reached by logic has ever convinced me as utterly or stirred me as deeply as did that red-tailed hawk."[9] Sanders's adamant faith in the truth of his experience is characteristic of those who have revelations, whether in the context of traditional or ecological conversion. The defining quality of such "convictional experiences," writes scholar James Loder, is the "imaginative leap to certainty."[10]

That certainty is not grasped by the mind so much as embraced and held by the heart. Moments of inspiration are—in the etymological sense—an inbreath of spirit. Their lucidity derives from a creative force that is more than personal; it is universal, even divine. Its full strength can manifest suddenly, as Rachel Carson attests, recounting how this force helped breathe spirit into one of her writing projects: "Later, listening to Beethoven, the mood became, I suppose, more creative, and rather suddenly I understood what the anthology should be—the story it should tell—the deep significance it might have. I suppose I can never explain it in words. . . . It was a mood of tremendous exaltation, I wept. I paced the floor." This experience, although deeply emotional, might not be considered revelatory were it not for Carson's conviction of its meaning. She concludes her description of the experience: "only when I have felt myself so deeply moved, so possessed by something outside myself, can I feel that inner confidence that what I am doing is right."[11]

For Carson, as for many converts, the spiritual power of revelation is felt so strongly that it appears to originate outside oneself. It moves—in the revelatory moment—from being transcendent to immanent, manifesting in a burst of creative energy. Its powerful presence, Carson suggests, awakens her inner confidence, helping to strengthen her ecological practice.

Ecological Awakenings

Convictional experiences such as those Carson and Sanders describe occur frequently among ecological writers and the general populace. In one survey, religious scholars found that 39 percent of respondents reported having had mystical experiences, many of them triggered by encounters in nature.[12] Anecdotal evidence from autobiographical narratives confirms the prevalence of crystalline moments. For centuries, nature writers have recorded glimpses of a reality wider and deeper than ordinary consciousness allows. Revelatory experiences recur so frequently in nature writing that they have become a hallmark of the genre—with such prominent examples as William Wordsworth's "intimations of immortality," Henry Thoreau's calls to awaken, John Muir's ecstatic encounters with "Nature-God," and Annie Dillard's visions of an illumined life. Ecological writers can be characterized as "prospectors for revelation," individuals who seek out numinous encounters and consciously sift through their experiences to locate valuable nuggets.[13] This prospecting may become an enduring avocation so that crystalline moments are collected like gems.

The form and character of each gem is different, reflecting the light of its setting. Revelations occur outdoors in both wild and domesticated settings, most often in places of natural beauty. They can even occur indoors, when the conscious mind is engaged in reading or disengaged in sleep. Given the broad range of precipitating factors, there is a surprising uniformity in the responses that revelations provoke: most people report experiencing great clarity, intensified sensual awareness, wonder, and a peaceful sense of belonging.

Revelatory moments can be critical turning points in the conversion process, shifting one's perspective markedly or confirming existing beliefs. For writers who already have a strong attachment to Earth, convictional experiences may renew their resolve to live out their spiritual vision.

The insight concentrated in these awakenings can redirect the course of a life. Moments of intense perception reveal in a sense more than is actually there. Intuition and imagination literally re-cognize (perceive anew) a reality that reason cannot fully grasp. Like the multisensory experiences children have, crystalline moments can imprint deeply on the heart. They often become guiding memories to which individuals return for perspective and reassurance.

A well-known example appears in Aldo Leopold's collection *A Sand County Almanac*. Recalling his early years as a forester when he was "full of trigger-itch," Leopold describes how he and colleagues responded to the sight of a mother wolf and cubs by "pumping lead into the pack . . . with more excitement than accuracy." The gunfire brought down the old wolf, and Leopold reached her "in time to watch a fierce green fire dying in her eyes. I realized then," he reflects, "and have known ever since, that there was something new to me in those eyes—something known only to her and to the mountain."[14] That incident marked the beginning of a profound shift in Leopold's attitude toward the natural world, moving him from a utilitarian perspective to a life-centered ethic where the human is not "conqueror of the land community . . . [but] plain member and citizen of it."[15] Leopold's glimpse of the wolf's deep knowing awakened an appreciation for the wisdom inherent in the natural world and occasioned a humility that came to inform his ecological philosophy and practice.

Revelations hold the power to break the surface of consciousness, sending ripples across the breadth of one's life. Writer Lynne Bama recounts how her life transformed in the wake of a profound insight she experienced during a visit to Wyoming:

> I had climbed the ridge intently, concentrating on my footing. Only when I got to the top did I turn around and discover that the clouds on the other side of the valley had blown away. What had

seemed to be a complete landscape had miraculously enlarged, and I found myself staring at an enormous volcanic rampart, its face streaked and marbled with veins of new-fallen snow.

I sat down on a rock, stunned by this unexpected, looming presence, by the eerie combination of nearness and deep space and silence. In that moment the shape of my life changed. Two years later I moved to Wyoming and have since lived nowhere else.[16]

Revelatory moments represent quantum leaps in perception, where one's vision is, as Bama suggests, miraculously enlarged. The ordinary appears extraordinary as one glimpses a new dimension of being. These experiences can extend one's understanding not only of self but of place. Returning after a quarter-century to the mountain ridge where her epiphany occurred, Bama reports being struck by the gulf "between what I knew then and what I know now."[17] That fleeting insight decades earlier sparked an ongoing quest to know the land in its entirety and learn from its stories. In the process, Bama moved—as Leopold did—from a vision of bountiful nature and unmarred beauty to a keen realization of how the surrounding ecosystem had been diminished. While this deeper awareness of place brought pain, it helped nurture her devotion to the land.

Revelations—often seen as momentary flashes of illumination—do not recede readily into the dark hollows of memory. The stories of Bama, Leopold, and other writers suggest that these insights imprint on the imagination and conscience, strengthening an ecological practice. They become standards by which to measure one's moral and spiritual evolution. The questions they occasion can reverberate within one for years. Leopold's insight, for example, spurred him to learn more about the wisdom that sustains a balanced and synergistic relationship between a species and its habitat. Crystalline moments that stretch ethical horizons can help individuals reconstitute their relation to the natural world.

Revelatory insights can also provide an ongoing source of inspiration, reaffirming one's faith in an indwelling mystery. Rather than turning to conventional creeds and texts for reassurance in difficult times, individuals may rely on the memory of a convictional experience. In this way, remembrance comes to reinforce the initial impact of a revelation.

Edward Abbey's first glimpse of canyon country had this salutary effect, remaining in his imagination through trying years of military service abroad: "through all the misery and tedium . . . of the war . . . I kept bright in my remembrance . . . what I had seen and felt—yes—and even smelled—on that one blazing afternoon on a freight train rolling across the Southwest." His train ride awakening, a fleeting but powerful glimpse of all that is "free, decent, sane, clean, and true," sustained Abbey's will to live through the war and lured him back to make a home in the Southwest.[18] That revelatory glimpse of canyon country came to nourish his commitment to place. Abbey later wrote that he had long looked for somewhere to take his stand: "Now that I think I've found it," he asserted, "I must defend it."[19] His ecological practice grew in large measure from his deepening devotion to desert country.

Callings

Revelatory insights can hold a sense of destiny, calling one toward possibilities not yet envisioned. The new paths that open may guide one's turn to Earth. Rachel Carson recounts an experience during college when she caught a fleeting glimpse of where her life would lead:

> Years ago on a night when rain and wind beat against the windows of my college dormitory room, a line from [Alfred Lord Tennyson's] "Locksley Hall" burned itself into my mind—"For the mighty wind arises, roaring seaward, and I go."
>
> I can still remember my intense emotional response as that line spoke to something within me seeming to tell me that my own path led to the sea—which I had never seen—and that my own destiny was somehow linked with the sea.

And so, as you know, it has been. When I finally became the sea's biographer, the sea brought me recognition and what the world calls success.[20]

Carson's momentary intuition demonstrates the improbable but potent power of revelations. By early childhood, she had developed a passion for the sea, reading all she could about this realm known to her only through books. Her epiphany in college confirmed the truth of that youthful passion, lending her confidence to embark on studies in marine biology (a path that college administrators strongly discouraged). She trusted her intuitive insight enough to disregard the advice of others and follow its mysterious calling to the sea.

Carson's account reflects what scholars have found among traditional religious converts: that many individuals experience a strong sense of being guided. This feeling may be particularly acute among ecological writers who attend carefully to both inner and outer worlds and the resonance between them. In what he terms "guiding moments," Scott Momaday has found circumstances that are "not accidental to me—they seem to me to be arranged in some pattern, like the pattern of the universe."[21] Momaday envisions a continual resonance between the physical world and our psychological and spiritual reality. This dynamic is what Carson alludes to when she describes herself as the sea's biographer: outer ecology, for her, is not a collection of objects but what Passionist priest Thomas Berry calls a community of subjects. The sea is a complex, multifarious character whose life story demands to be told.

Like Carson and Abbey, writer Gary Paul Nabhan experienced a strong sense of calling in late adolescence. He had dropped out of high school and was working outdoors to repair tracks at the local steel mill. One day he glanced up to see six blue herons flying low through the grimy air. He watched them circle as if looking for a stopover site. Finding only shallow ponds beside slag heaps, they slowly flew on. Nabhan's heart went with them, he recalls: "I felt welling up within me a profound desire to know those birds better."

That experience illumined a vocational path Nabhan had never considered. Turning from the railroad work his father and uncles had done, he began training himself as a naturalist. He felt guided and affirmed in his choice by that enduring vision. The improbability of a crystalline moment happening in that sooty scene made it all the more persuasive for Nabhan: "Even in the most damaged of habitats, in the drudgery of the most menial labor, whatever wildlife remained could still pull at me deeply enough to disrupt business-as-usual."[22]

The prevalence of ecological awakenings late in adolescence echoes a pattern identified by religious scholars in which most conventional conversions occur during adolescence.[23] Few scholars speculate as to why revelations occur with such frequency in young adulthood, but it may coincide with developmental needs to establish a vocational direction or with the spiritual questions that accompany the consolidation of one's identity. Ecological converts experience revelations throughout adulthood, but their awakenings in adolescence seem particularly critical in directing their turns to Earth.

Insights that occur later in life may build upon earlier revelations, extending a sense of ecological connection over space and time. The sense of dwelling within an unfolding evolutionary story appears most strongly among Native American writers whose "tribal sense of self [is] as a moving event in a moving universe."[24] Scott Momaday attributes this dynamic perspective to the profound bond that joins native people to sacred lands. In holy places, he writes, ones touches "the pulse of the living planet. . . . You become one with a spirit that pervades geologic time, that indeed confounds time and space."[25] In many native belief systems, evolution *is* revelation. The turning of seasons, the movement of stars, the cycles of growth and decay all reveal a sacred presence. The divine, in this view, is not unveiled in rare moments, an occasional gem along one's path. Instead, the numinous manifests in countless forms every time one recognizes or creates what Latin Americans call *milagro pequeño*, a small miracle or holy moment.[26]

Honoring the unfolding mystery moment by moment can lead

to a new view of spiritual identity, what philosopher Alfred North
Whitehead terms "process theology." Akin to Native American perspectives, it conceives the world as a dynamic web of infinite interconnections. Spirit infuses the unfolding pattern of being, making
God—as writer Mary Daly observed—more aptly a verb than a
noun. Without deliberate theological study, many ecological writers
seem to arrive intuitively at a process view of the divine.

[handwritten margin note: turn over a nick + you shall find NE St Thoms?]

Different Divinities

Those who turn to Earth tend to rely on their own unmediated experience outdoors as a source of divine revelation, resisting the
hierarchical structure and authoritarian stance of most formal religions. They affirm their conviction of spiritual belonging through
personal experience rather than collective doctrines or creeds. "I
sensed this permeating presence before I learned any religious language to speak of it," Scott Russell Sanders reflects, "and I sense it
still, after I have grown wary of all the names for God."[27] Communion with the natural world affords symbols and rituals to sustain a
faith not bound by institutional religion.

Seeking the divine within nature, many contemporary ecological
writers part ways with their nineteenth-century predecessors who
read the natural world in metaphorical terms (looking for signs of a
transcendent God). Edward Abbey strongly objected to the traditional view that the elements of nature symbolize a distant deity:
"That land, those mountains, those canyons and rivers," he wrote,
"you don't get religion from them; they are religion."[28] The conversion he sought was not to a lone creator God but directly to the
divinity of creation. Abbey found spirit dwelling within the myriad
forms of matter about him, living and nonliving. "If I have a religion," he conceded, "it's pantheism, the belief that everything is in
some sense holy, or divine, or sacred."[29]

Writers who hold this view experience their time outdoors as an
immersion in the sacred. Alaskan writer Richard Nelson stresses
that this sacramental experience of Earth is not symbolic or repre-

sentational. It is a vivid, sensual confirmation of the spiritual: "Anyone in the forest can partake directly of sacredness, experience
sacredness with his entire body, breathe sacredness and contain it
within himself, drink the sacred water as a living communion . . .
open his eyes and witness the burning beauty of sacredness."[30]
Immersion in the natural world, Nelson suggests, is by definition a
spiritual baptism.

The pantheistic view that Nelson and Abbey hold is less common
among ecological writers than panentheism, which sees the divine
as *simultaneously* transcendent and immanent.[31] Many writers
favor the perspective of preservationist writer John Muir: "All of the
individual 'things' or 'beings' into which the world is wrought," he
observes, "are sparks of the Divine Soul variously clothed upon with
flesh, leaves, or that harder tissue called rock."[32] Panentheists hold
an inclusive view of the divine as illuminating every being—both
living creatures and elemental matter. Their deity represents the
unity that dwells within multiplicity. Alice Walker captures the far-
reaching stretch of this theological view: "God is everything that is,
ever was or ever will be."[33] The divine force envisioned by panentheists is present in the unfolding drama of everyday life. God, or
the Great Mystery, dwells in the *milagros pequeños*.

For some writers, the small miracles and holy moments recur so
frequently that they no longer seem extraordinary. Revelation becomes (as in many indigenous cultures) a common phenomenon,
one dependent on a "devotional practice" of sensory attunement to
outer and inner terrain. The body acts as a spiritual tuning fork, a
means of finding harmony and resonance with all the dimensions of
being within and around one.[34]

Cultivating an embodied spiritual practice can reinforce a turn to
Earth. Conversion brings us to our senses, literally and figuratively.
By listening and seeing with the whole body, we can attend to the
spirit that inheres in the world. "I don't know exactly what a prayer
is," poet Mary Oliver confesses, but "I do know how to pay attention."[35] The art of deep attention can become a means of worship
even when one has no formal religious rites.

In learning to be attentive, ecological writers often draw inspiration from their literary predecessors: an interest in the "psychological phenomenon of awareness has characterized ecological writing for centuries."[36] Generations of writers have found that careful scrutiny reveals the intricate connections holding together the whole, bonds that are at once real and intangible, mundane and magical. To sense these connections, individuals need to relinquish purposeful activity at times—consciously becoming still, humble, and free of expectation. A stance of deliberate nonattachment can be hard for Westerners who are conditioned to analyze experience and to focus on doing rather than being. In their quest to attain these ideals, some writers turn for guidance to Eastern and indigenous cultures and to mystical traditions.

Rachel Carson, for example, was strongly influenced by Albert Schweitzer, an Alsatian-born medical doctor whose ethic of "reverence for life" grew from his study of comparative religions and time spent in African tribal villages. Schweitzer's own philosophical vision crystallized in an epiphanic moment after days of intensive concentration. Traveling by boat along an African river one evening, his attention drifted to a herd of hippopotamuses wading in the water. As he watched them, the word *Ehrfurcht* came into his mind "unforeseen and unsought," an experience he described as an iron door yielding. *Ehrfurcht*, commonly translated as "reverence for life," actually connotes a harder-edged awe—a wonder tinged with humility and even fear.[37] It holds echoes of the sublime, acknowledging forces beyond human control.

This concept has influenced many ecological writers because it captures the essence of the revelatory moment—an experience of awe before the mystery of being, tempered by an enduring sense of humility. Those who pursue an ecological practice often report that wonder in the world's complementary diversity undermines their capacity to act heedlessly or selfishly. "Reverence for life" speaks to both the spiritual and moral dimensions of a conversion to Earth, recognizing that devout attention constitutes a lived form of prayer and a call to conscience.

The creative process can reinforce an abiding reverence for life. "The discipline of the writer," Rachel Carson observes, "is to learn to be still and listen to what his subject has to tell him."[38] She underscores the vital need for humility and patient attention, acknowledging the sacredness of one's subject. The writing process is a devotional practice like prayer, Carson implies, a means of listening to the voiceless dimensions of being. When one's subject is fraught with mystery and paradox, this practice can prove difficult. Both in her books on the sea and in *Silent Spring*, Carson faced the challenge of sharing a complex and ambiguous subject. The creative strength of her work derives from her capacity to attend simultaneously to outer and inner worlds, articulating the correspondence between them.

One way that writers attend to the inner world is by consciously recalling images and visions from dreams. Many readily acknowledge the transformational force of dreams, even though they cannot explain their source or form: "I have powerful dreams," Scott Momaday affirms, "and I believe they determine who I am and what I do. But how, I'm not sure. Maybe that is how it ought to be. Mystery is, perhaps, the necessary condition of dreams."[39]

That sense of internal mystery can foster humility, a willingness to acknowledge how little of life we can fathom. Edward Abbey recalls a dream that left him with "an afterglow of sweetness and happiness," then speculates that it may not have been a dream at all: "Indeed, it might have been the opposite—an awakening. A brief awakening that slips through my grasp, elusive as a rainbow of light, when I try to cling to it."[40] Other writers also explore this liminal realm where dreams draw one into a larger reality. They let go of the dualism between waking and sleeping consciousness in favor of an "awakened" life that joins conscious and unconscious wisdom. The only way to remain awake, they suggest, is to pay attention to inner and outer terrain and the dialogue of dreams that joins them.

Repercussions of Revelation

Revelatory moments can be critical junctures in a turn to Earth because they reconstitute relations between inner and outer ecology, transforming perception and identity. A crystalline moment evokes wonder and humility before the mystery of creation and renews a spiritual faith in the unfolding pattern of being. As the accounts in this chapter illustrate, many individuals interpret their revelations as guiding their conversions to Earth.

Experiencing the sacredness of the world in vivid moments of insight can move one to take moral action: "what the transforming moment does," scholar James Loder explains, "is place people inside their convictions."[41] It grounds their morality and theology in the heartfelt experience of ecological interconnection rather than in philosophical theories or religious doctrines. The writers in this work testify that contact with Earth's sacredness can open the way to new modes of thinking and living.

One Reader's Revelation

I grew up with a strong but unconventional faith. Our family did not attend church: what we might have sought in a faith community—words of inspiration and solace, the company of fellow seekers, the comfort of ritual—we found instead in books. Our pilgrimages were not to holy shrines but to used bookstores where we pored over shelves for hours, delighting in works known and unknown. The walls of our house were peopled with literary companions for readers of every age.

Coming from this background, I trusted in the power of book learning. I loved to research new topics, particularly those that crossed disciplines. Finding common threads in markedly different works gave me a deep sense of the inherent unity within people and the world at large.

When pondering weighty questions, I turned to books for answers or at least for illumination. Seeking guidance on ways to revitalize our ties to the ecological whole, I pored over religious, philosophical, literary, and environmental texts. During a prolonged time of intensive and solitary study, I broke away from books periodically to indulge a passion for sea kayaking that dated back to college. Having first learned the sport as a form of recreation, I now pursued it as more of a spiritual practice, a kind of re-creation. It immersed me in the elemental world of wind and water.

Initially, kayaking simply afforded a ready means of retreat—providing a few hours on the water to regain perspective. As I grew more experienced, though, I wanted to take extended trips. With a friend, I set about planning a three-week trek along the Maine coast in which we would camp on islands that permitted overnight visitors. We set out with gear and six days' worth of food and water filling every ounce of volume our two boats held. While prepared in many respects for the adventure (in terms of skills, gear, and physical fitness), I was wholly unprepared for the way this extended immersion in the elements would touch my heart.

Away from the relentless bustle of human activity, the ubiquitous hum of motors and tick of clocks, we sank into a rhythm set by sun, moon, wind, and tide. Joining in this ancient dance led us out of chronological time and into a realm where we could sense the pulse of life in everything around us.

One morning we awoke to pea-soup fog. Donning our wetsuits, we packed up and set out, navigating by compass. There was no wind, so the water's surface was smooth and almost iridescent, like the pearly lining of an oyster shell. As we passed through a quiet narrows between two islands, barely visible through the fog, a heavy rain began to fall. Each large drop turned to a silver bead as it hit the water surface, splashed up, and fell again. Our paddling slowed and then stopped as we sat transfixed by this sparkling dance of opalescent drops showering on and around us. It was a blessing, a baptism into a world older and wiser than the one we thought we had known.

That trip was a long, glistening chain of *milagros pequeños*, moments of embodied connection that deepened my love for the coast and my commitment to sustain its integrity. For the first time, I visited many islands that I had read and even written about but never actually seen. Walking their cobble and sand beaches and their fir-scented forest paths, I began to sense the vital dimensions of being that words could never capture. My faith in words, I came to realize, rests on a broader and stronger spiritual base. What propels my turn to Earth and fuels my ecological practice are experiences of *contact* with the world (as Thoreau put it in a revelatory moment on Maine's Mount Katahdin), when I bask in the beneficence of being. Words recall revelatory experiences, giving me stories to live by, but they can never substitute for the moment-to-moment vitality of participating in the greater whole.

This realization changed the course of my research. I turned away from theoretical works and began to focus on the firsthand accounts of individuals who had come to center their lives on Earth. In place of abstract analysis about our estrangement from the natural world, I found vivid testimonials affirming a new vision of ecological connection.

5

Reciprocity

A covenant of mutual regard and responsibility binds me
together with the forest. We share in a common nurturing.
—Richard K. Nelson, *The Island Within*

Ecological converts seek to foster the well-being of the greater
whole through a reciprocal exchange that honors the "evocative resonance among things," the life energy that animates all beings and
the elemental world.[1] Sensing this existential web of connection can
deepen a convert's ecological practice and foster a moral resolve to
"share in a common nurturing."

By acknowledging their existential reciprocity, ecological converts counter dominant cultural tenets—challenging both the capi-
talistic drive to exploit natural resources and biblical injunctions
to subdue and dominate other beings. More fundamentally, they
counter Western society's adamant and entrenched individualism.
Refusal to acknowledge the promise and constraints of interdependence exacerbates many ecological ills, from runoff water pollution
to global warming. Individuals pursue actions that appear to be in
their self-interest, not stopping to consider that if everyone else
follows a similar course, they will devastate collective habitats. Elements of the natural world that are not defined by property bound-

aries (such as the air, oceans, and groundwater) are most vulnerable to this unwitting exploitation by individuals—a destructive sequence that sociologist Garret Hardin terms the "tragedy of the commons."

Those who turn to Earth strive to resist this corrosive individualism by honoring their kinship with other creatures. The animals, plants, and elemental matter that share their terrain come to represent neighbors with common needs and concerns. By extending their sense of community across species lines, ecological converts deepen their commitment to sustain the good of the greater whole.

Awaking Empathy

A profound encounter with another creature can close the chasm that typically divides humans from other animals, offering what Rachel Carson termed an "intuitive comprehension of the whole life."[2] Empathic understanding confers on each being the status of a valued subject, a creature of intrinsic worth rather than an incidental accessory or backdrop. The bond forged in this meeting is not one of union, a complete merging of identity, but of spiritual communion. By relinquishing psychological defenses, a person can momentarily share the experience of a creature who is incontrovertibly other and yet kin. This communion does not stem from projection or anthropomorphizing (seeing an animal in human terms so that its experience becomes intelligible) but rather from an extension of feeling that appears to be instinctual.

Stories of empathic encounters with other animals fill the annals of nature writing. These exchanges can hold revelatory power, imprinting themselves on heart and memory for life. Anthropologist and writer Loren Eiseley recalls a brief dance he shared with an African crane at the Philadelphia Zoo. The bird—being "under the impulse of spring" and recognizing in Eiseley a creature of appropriate vertical height—"made some intricate little steps" in his direction and extended its wings. Eiseley tried to match the bird's sophisticated courtship dance: "I extended my arms, fluttered and flapped them. After looking carefully . . . to verify that we were alone, I executed what I hoped was the proper enticing shuffle and jigged about in a circle. So did my partner. We did this a couple of times with mounting enthusiasm when I happened to see a park policeman sauntering in our direction." Eiseley felt he had to abandon the dance, walking away with studied nonchalance under the policeman's watchful gaze. Reflecting back on the encounter decades later, Eiseley notes that his exchange with the crane "supersedes in vividness years of graduate study."[3] That momentary meeting of unlikely partners in an ancient dance touched Eiseley's soul at a level beneath cognition.

Numerous writers attest to having similar experiences of profound and unexpected communion with other species. As Rachel Carson traversed a beach one night, her flashlight beam surprised a small ghost crab—silent amidst "the all-enveloping, primeval sounds" of wind and water. Carson had seen hundreds of ghost crabs in other settings, yet she reports: "suddenly I was filled with the odd sensation that for the first time I knew the creature in its own world—that I understood, as never before, the essence of its being." Understanding, in this sense, comes closer to mystical identification than to rational knowledge. Such a meeting across species lines can hold an air of enchantment: "In that moment time was suspended," Carson writes, "the world to which I belonged did not exist."[4] Entering the dark and primeval realm of this lone crustacean, she momentarily relinquishes her ordinary reality, falling into what T. S. Eliot calls "time not our time," an elemental world in which humans play no part.

Encounters that unveil extraordinary dimensions of being can hold a fairy-tale quality that makes them seem implausible. Social norms dictate that sane adults do not dance with cranes or drop into deep timelessness. Yet writers hold to the truth of their experiences, refusing to dismiss them as inconsequential fantasy. Even those with rigorous scientific backgrounds like Carson and Eiseley readily relinquish that analytical view in the face of compelling connections with other beings. Their encounters remind them of a reciprocal

relation to animals that the larger culture has all but lost. Glimps-
ing the essence of another creature, they sense the potential for a
life where such exchanges would not be anomalous but routine.

The power of these encounters can extend beyond the initial
moment, reverberating in heart and imagination through the sort
of kinesthetic imprinting that children experience—recollections
held as much in body as in mind. Converts may literally incorporate
their experience of connection so that it becomes part of their identity, continually reminding them of their own animal nature and
kinship with all life.

Cultivating Reciprocity

Vivid experiences of communion between species suggest the presence of a powerful bond that joins diverse forms of life. Scientists
Stephen Kellert and E. O. Wilson call this innate affinity for other
creatures "biophilia" and suggest that it may be strongly encoded in
humans. Whether or not it is genetically programmed, biophilia
may help build the imaginative bridge that enables humans to em-
pathize with other creatures.

Scott Russell Sanders crossed this bridge while in the wild Boundary Waters region watching a family of otters at play. Seeing the exuberant creatures awakened Sanders's interest in their experience of
otterness. He sought to "feel the world for a spell through their
senses, to think otter thoughts." That desire to connect, Sanders
asserts, holds redemptive power: "the yearning to leap across the distance, the reaching out in imagination to a fellow creature, seems to
me a worthy impulse, perhaps the most encouraging and distinctive
one we have."[5] Biophilia is not only a particular gift of humans, he
suggests, but a potential moral resource. It can help close the gap that
divides us from the rest of life by cultivating a greater capacity for
empathy and compassion.

An impulse to identify with other species can be thwarted, though,
by rational arguments, cultural taboos, and emotional conditioning.

The prevailing scientific worldview leaves little room for experiences that cannot be verified by empirical analysis: profound encounters with other species tend to be dismissed as flights of the imagination or products of a writer's "artistic license." Moments of mystical connection challenge the dominant cultural practice of defining identity in opposition to others. One literary critic observes, for example, that a "facile sense of harmony, even identity, with one's surroundings . . . would fail to produce self-awareness of any depth or vividness."[6] Any alliance with "one's surroundings" is seen as threatening the autonomous self. Those less influenced by Western intellectual traditions, in contrast, often believe that self-awareness *depends* on identity with one's environment because the self is inseparable from place.

The chance to meet another creature on its terms can also be blocked by inbred fears. Whether culturally imposed or warranted by genuine risk, fears may come to overtake sympathy. Even writers devoted to the natural world find their appreciation for other life forms qualified at times. Alice Walker was raised to believe that snakes are "dangerous, frightful, repulsive, [and] sinister."[7] This early conditioning has endured, despite Walker's cognitive knowledge that many snakes are harmless and her spiritual conviction that they are entitled to life. When a snake took up residence in Walker's garden, her abiding fear won out over reason and compassion, and she allowed a friend to kill it. Walker felt guilty for having the snake destroyed, though, and has let subsequent ones remain. Her struggle is emblematic of the challenges converts face trying to realize the ideal of reciprocity. In a culture marked by deep-seated fears of what is natural and wild, those who seek to practice reciprocity must challenge societal assumptions and work through personal fears.

Terry Tempest Williams confronts her fears through deliberate immersion in desert habitats, unforgiving settings whose aridity, barrenness, and extreme temperatures deter most forms of life. She faces the risks of this region consciously, having been scarred by canyon rock and threatened by the turbulent waters of flash floods.

The ever-present dangers do not diminish Williams's love for the desert. They deepen it. The desert's unpredictable otherness draws her: to love the fierce and spontaneous energy of a wild place is for her the essence of an ecological practice. A reciprocal exchange, she implies, need not be tame and cultivated. It can celebrate the wildness without and within.

Both Williams and Walker hold that the strongest forms of kinship embrace difference and wildness. Reciprocity calls humans into relation with *all* species, not merely with those that are "useful" or "beautiful." Wary of the culture's penchant for natural settings sanitized of any unpleasant or threatening elements, they suggest that kinship not be confined to cute and cuddly species (cherishing otters, for example, over snakes). They seek to acknowledge all forms of otherness, even when their admiration is tempered by fear. In this way, reciprocity becomes a spiritual discipline, a consistent effort to extend the reach of one's compassion.

Individuals who seek a deeper kinship with life must contend not only with innate fears but also with cultural taboos that discourage sensory contact with other beings. As Eiseley found in his dance with the crane, one must look about carefully before such exchanges and abandon them in the presence of other humans. Western culture encourages people to treat the natural world as an aesthetic realm, a gallery where one may look but not touch. Physical contact is deemed appropriate only for utilitarian purposes: gardening, pruning and harvesting plants, or rewarding domesticated animals. Any physical expression of caring that extends beyond these roles tends to be ridiculed, as evident in the common epithet "tree-hugger."

In their quest to foster reciprocity, some converts consciously flout these strictures. Scott Russell Sanders takes obvious satisfaction in challenging such taboos: "I do hug trees. . . . I hum beside creeks, hoot back at owls, lick rocks, smell flowers, rub my hands over the grain in wood. I'm well aware that such behavior makes me seem weird in the eyes of people who've become disconnected from the Earth. But in the long evolutionary perspective, they're the anomaly."[8] Sanders reasserts his right to participate fully within nature based on evolutionary precedent. Humans have not evolved beyond kinship, he argues; they need to continually affirm their physical bonds with the natural whole.

One way to deepen that affinity is through empathic participation in the food web. Identifying with other animals and plants does not preclude harvesting or consuming them. What reciprocity does require is an appreciation for the sacramental nature of consumption and a commitment to treat fellow beings—even those one kills—with respect and gratitude. Richard Nelson, a writer who supports his family by subsistence hunting and fishing, reflects on the conflict inherent in his role: "how strange it is to love so deeply what gives you life," he writes, "and to feel such pleasure and such pain in taking from that source."[9] Conscious participation in the food web can foster a strong sense of humility, where gratitude for the life that sustains one rests alongside the recognition that one's own chance to nourish other life will invariably come. In a world where all life feeds on other life, "we too will be offerings—we are all edible."[10]

The practice of reciprocity is fraught with paradox, perched precariously between honoring life and extinguishing it. Every being, Albert Schweitzer observed, represents a "life which wills to live in the midst of life which wills to live."[11] Recognizing this dynamic, ecological writers urge that use of other species be grounded not simply in respect for their rights but in a spirit of profound reverence for their lives and gratitude for their sacrifice.

A Web of Dependencies

Reciprocity counters the dominant utilitarian ethic by suggesting that a single moral baseline governs all interactions within and beyond the human community. Any attempt to hold different standards, caring for some while exploiting others, ignores the essential reciprocity that enables our existence. Respect and care are part of the "common nurturing" that sustains all life: in Edward Abbey's words, humans should offer other life—and the planet itself—"the same generosity and tolerance we require from our fellow humans."[12]

Converts who strive to extend their practice of compassion often conclude that while one may embrace the planet in heart and imagination, meaningful action is not feasible on so vast a scale. Ethicist Nel Noddings observes that care involves an exchange between individuals; it cannot be given to generalized groups of others.[13] A conscious practice of reciprocity, by recognizing each particular being, avoids the pitfalls of philosophical abstractions and political generalities that disregard individuals or deny differences among them.

Mindful encounters with other beings can foster a morality grounded in empathy rather than monolithic principles. The standard governing behavior becomes one of response-ability, the sustained capacity for attention and care. Love is "a kind of readiness," poet Duane Big Eagle writes: "The little decisions / make a vision / by which we come to live."[14] An empathic mode of relation reveals the unique qualities of each being and the web of communities that binds together the whole.

Ecological writers seek to honor these communal ties, advocating for an ethic of kinship to replace the prevailing ethos of competitive individualism. They challenge the entrenched hierarchical view that places humans "over" animals and land, believing that we do not dwell *on* the Earth so much as *within* it: we are "the belongings of the world, not the owners."[15] The encompassing natural community in which we participate recognizes none of the proprietary rights that we have asserted. An ideal relation, Scott Momaday suggests, would be one of "reciprocal appropriation," in which people invest themselves in the land and simultaneously incorporate the land into their "most fundamental experience."[16] That reciprocal exchange, a guiding practice among many tribal peoples, seeks to sustain the well-being of each participant without sacrificing the interests of the larger community.

A Partnership with Place

Many ecological converts deepen their ties with other species by devoting themselves to a particular region, simultaneously learning from the land and caring for it. Place becomes more than a physical setting or social unit, an element of outer ecology. It begins to shape inner ecology, transforming perception and identity.

To foster a partnership with place, some ecological writers "apprentice" themselves to home ground, learning natural and cultural history from native people, from books, and, most important, from the land itself (through such means as field sketching, photography, tracking, and ecological restoration). Indigenous people have a relation to the land that extends back generations, providing a wealth of accumulated stories and a tribal sense of kinship. Outside this context, it can be harder to cultivate a sustained link with the land. For someone living in a transient and fast-paced society, "it is a spiritual discipline to root the mind in a particular landscape."[17] That discipline requires one to accept limits, adapting to the region's topographic, climatological, and ecological constraints and declining opportunities that would uproot one.

Committing oneself to place can dislodge old patterns of belief and nurture new perspectives. Psychologist Thomas Moore describes it as a move "from a mental to an erotic view of ecology— erotic in the sense that our longing, attachment and intimacy with place is considered more important than abstract ideas or ideals."[18] Converts' accounts confirm Moore's observation. They describe their bonds with place as both erotic and covenantal, encompassing many elements vital to a thriving marriage: a commitment to mutual nourishment; fidelity; and a capacity for growth and improvisation. Loving a place, writer Richard Nelson suggests, is akin to loving a person: "it only develops through a long process of intimacy, commitment and devotion."[19] The commitment made by long-term inhabitants of a place allows for an unparalleled depth of understanding and for continual transformation in the context of stability.

Over time, converts may come to ground their faith in home terrain. Eudora Welty describes her homeland in the South as "my source of knowledge. It tells me the important things," she asserts: "It steers me and keeps me going straight. . . . It saves me."[20] Welty's account suggests that place can shape a personal credo. Her bond with the land and its life community is not a secondary influence on Welty: she names it her primary source of knowledge, a sacred force that steers and saves her. Other writers express similar sentiments, acknowledging that their native ground provides spiritual insight and direction. Terry Tempest Williams consciously forfeits Mormon dogma in favor of wildness, confirming her allegiance to the land: "to deny one's genealogy with the earth," she writes, is "to commit treason against one's soul."[21]

In the reciprocal exchange between person and place, what one receives from the natural community corresponds to what one offers it in care and attention. Rather than being a static, material construct, place represents a dynamic dance of interrelated beings. The thoughts and actions of each resident therefore determine the quality of place. "Sacred ground is in some way earned," Scott Momaday writes. "It is consecrated, made holy with offerings—song and ceremony, joy and sorrow, the dedication of mind and heart."[22] Through ritual arts and a devoted ecological practice, individuals can recreate holy ground (a theme developed in chapter 7).

Humility

Conscious efforts to renew place can come to transform our moral and spiritual geography. "The more you engage with the land," writer John Tallmadge observes, "the more willing you are to let it change you."[23] Reciprocity fosters ethical action by calling forth compassion (literally the capacity to "feel with" other beings). "Feeling is the basic bodily ingredient that mediates our connectedness to the world," ethicist Beverly Harrison suggests: so to be "effective moral agents" we must know what we feel.[24] A practice of reciprocity cultivates an empathic identification with other beings and the elemental Earth that can prompt a deepened sense of moral accountability.

Scott Momaday, for example, describes how the light pollution affecting his home region is not just an environmental problem but an ethical concern. He fears that his children will be deprived of the opportunity he had as a child to watch stars, and that they may lose the accompanying tribal stories. This prospect, Momaday states, "threatens me at my center. The stars are very important to me mythically. To think of losing the stars represents to me a very deep wound."[25] When one identifies deeply with a place, degradation of the land is felt as a violation of self.

The widespread loss in modern industrial culture of a vital empathy with other beings has produced a moral negligence that endangers the ecological whole. Western society has succumbed to a fateful hubris, Rachel Carson asserted, losing a sense of its rightful place within nature: we fail "to see ourselves as a very tiny part of a vast and incredible universe, a universe that is distinguished above all else by a mysterious and wonderful unity that we flout at our peril."[26] In Carson's view, we place far too much faith in our own technological wizardry and do not honor the greater wisdom of ecological systems. She feared that this classic demonstration of hubris would lead (as in ancient myths) to fiery tragedy. Subsequent writers have echoed Carson's call for humility, citing further evidence of humans' physical and psychic dependence on the natural whole. Cultural historian Theodore Roszak calls the denial of this dependence the "epidemic psychosis of our time."[27] Only by acknowledging our existential state of reciprocity, he suggests, can we cure this life-threatening ailment.

Knowing that it will take considerable time to heal the larger society, converts take action where they can—each one cultivating an ecological practice grounded in humility. They try to live lightly within the larger web of life, treating other species with abiding respect. Even small gestures, such as carrying trapped insects outdoors or burying road-killed animals, can reinforce reciprocity. Over time, many converts move from quiet gestures of compassion to more public expressions of their links with the living land.

One Reader's Reciprocity

My commitment to work for the Earth stems, in large measure, from the profound touch of one particular place. The island that sparked my imagination and opened my senses in childhood has grown more central to my life and identity with each passing year. During my senior year of college, I visited the island alone for the first time and spent three days in a near constant state of revelation. It was October, and low light lent a vital glow to every tree, rock, and shrub, as if illuminating the spirit within. Amid the mottled brown grasses and shrubs were brilliant bits of color—scarlet sumac and rosehips tucked amidst saffron leaves. Having experienced the island before only in summer's bold light, I was wholly unprepared for the subtle but intense aura of autumn. I wandered about with senses and heart wide open, transfixed to find a whole new dimension of being within a place I thought I had known.

Since then I have returned to the island for countless "solo" stays. I use the term advisedly since the visits have been solitary only in the most narrow sense. The lack of human fellowship is more than made up for by intimate communion with other species, the chance to participate more fully in their elemental world.

On a solitary visit late one May, I spotted a seal pup about halfway down the beach, moving slowly and awkwardly toward the water. It is not unusual to find young seal pups at that season, languishing on the shore while their mothers are off feeding. Yet this one appeared to be injured or deformed. He (she?) moved without using his flippers to propel him. I watched his awkward gait from a distance, touched by his determination. When the pup finally reached the water, he wallowed for a moment, slowly circling his sleek cylindrical body. First one and then a second flipper emerged from his side, and he looked down at them, befuddled. The flippers made a few feeble strokes, and his expression changed. Even from a distance, I could see the light come on as he realized the purpose of these appendages.

I knew in that moment that I had just witnessed this wee creature's first trip to the sea. Wanting to honor his birth day journey, I ran back to get my camera. When I returned, the pup was still in a foot or two of water, rolling and twisting about with more assurance and grace. I approached slowly, not wanting to scare him. Far from being frightened, the pup appeared delighted to see me. He moved toward me in the water and began to haul himself up the beach, now putting his newfound flippers to good use. He began making soft bleating sounds, and I realized—with a rush of joy and trepidation—that this guileless little mammal was fully prepared to imprint on me. His mother had gone off to fish and he was ready to nurse. To him, I must have seemed like a reasonable stand-in—being of the right gender and zoological class. Not wanting to mislead him further, I backed off quickly so that his real mother could return and give him the nourishment he sought.

Rarely in life have I experienced such complete openness and trust in a wild animal. In that brief exchange, I glimpsed the possibility of a connection to other creatures not shrouded on their side by well-founded fear. Clearly they are not born wary and distrustful any more than humans are born vicious or cruel. If these behaviors are learned, on both sides, then we might forge a new basis for relating—one that honors the essential kinship that even a newborn can recognize.

6

Resistance

My heart is moved by all I cannot save:
so much has been destroyed.

I have to cast my lot with those
who age after age, perversely,

with no extraordinary power,
reconstitute the world.

—Adrienne Rich, "Natural Resources"

Turning *to* Earth requires turning *from* many of the beliefs and practices that dominate Western society. Ecological converts come to envision their lives as a "counter-friction" (in Thoreau's words), helping to slow the engines of industrial culture.[1] They exert this force through writing and acts of resistance such as lobbying, protesting, and civil disobedience. These measures extend an ecological practice from a private affirmation of interconnection to an active testimony, a declaration of one's spiritual and moral allegiance to Earth. Acting upon conscience, individuals "moved by all [they] cannot save" become motivated to save all they can.

The impulse to resist ecological degradation is often fueled as much by experiences of joy and kinship as by grief or guilt. Ecopsychologists have found that when individuals take environmental action "in direct response to a strengthening bond with the land, it leads to more substantial and pervasive change than that induced by moral condemnation and other types of external coercion."[2] The previous chapter provides anecdotal support for this claim, demonstrating how writers' growing attachment to place shapes and sustains their ecological practice.

Few converts credit technical information with propelling their turns to Earth, even when the content is alarming and the presentation evocative. Their accounts confirm Aldo Leopold's observation that an ethical response to the land depends upon an affective connection of love and understanding. Moments of remembrance, reflection, revelation, and reciprocity appear more likely to spur moral action than do reports or research findings.

A commitment to societal resistance appears to grow slowly over the course of a turn to Earth, as one moves from a casual appreciation for the natural world to an abiding devotion. With Henry Thoreau, for example, "nature was initially more a pastime. . . . Increasingly it became the environment in which he felt most comfortable. Then it became an occupation [both literary and botanical] . . . and finally a cause.[3] Rachel Carson followed a similar progression, going from a recreational interest in bird-watching and beachcombing to a career in science writing, and finally to a wholehearted engagement in environmental advocacy. Carson came to feel, in her words, "bound by a solemn obligation to do what I could. If I didn't at least try I could never again be happy in nature."[4] Converts may feel the need for active resistance so acutely that it seems to be a spiritual calling, a powerful summons deriving from a source beyond rational explanation. Efforts to resist such directives may prove futile, as Carson learned.

She was planning a book on evolution when a letter arrived seeking her help in alerting people to the dangers of pesticides. Knowing that this would be a discouraging and controversial topic, Carson sought out another writer for the task. Unable to find one, she conceded to draft a single magazine article. Despite her status as a bestselling author, three magazines rejected the proposed article. Finally, Carson's conscience compelled her to bring forth a full book on the topic, sacrificing her personal interests to serve the larger community. "Knowing the facts as I did," she reflected, "I could not rest until I had brought them to public attention."[5]

After committing herself to the task, Carson persisted despite a series of debilitating illnesses and personal setbacks. Her resolution is characteristic of those writers who decide to act upon their ecological convictions: once having adopted a cause, they tend not to relinquish it. They may experience cycles of dormancy and activism, but rarely do they retreat into complacency or censor themselves. Conscience impels them to express their moral convictions.

Against the Grain

In resisting environmental destruction, ecological converts must confront what is second nature to them—their most fundamental ways of seeing and knowing. The dominant intellectual traditions in Western culture can undermine an ecological practice, cleaving humans from nature, reason from emotion, spirit from matter, and life from death. This dualistic legacy conditions people to see the world as a collection of discrete and often opposing objects rather than as a dynamic interplay of related beings. The stories in chapter 3 illustrate how ecological converts raised in this tradition can be caught between their felt experience of interrelation and a prevailing worldview that validates only rational objectivity. Many of them resist the dominant tradition by consciously embracing dualisms and revaluing aesthetic, affective, and intuitive modes of knowing.

Rachel Carson, for example, challenged the cultural bias toward factual, objective knowledge, insisting that rational and empirical approaches to environmental change be complemented by what feminist psychologists term an "intimacy and equality between self and object" (rather than separation and mastery).[6] When one withholds judgment and empathically enter another's frame of reference, understanding becomes as much a mode of relation as a form of knowing. Carson describes how sensual and imaginal participation in lives of other beings enriched her perspective on the marine world: "To understand the shore it is not enough to catalogue its life. Understanding comes only when, standing on a beach, we can sense the long rhythms of earth and sea that sculptured its land forms . . . ; when we can sense with the eye and ear of the mind the surge of life beating always at its shores—blindly, inexorably pressing for a foothold. To understand the life of the shore, it is not enough to pick up an empty shell and say 'This is a murex,' or 'That is an angel wing.' True understanding demands intuitive comprehension of the whole life of the creature."[7] What is essential, Carson holds, is not the Linnaean impulse to label other life-forms but rather the art of opening wide our senses and imaginations. She underscores the need for a form of knowing often denigrated in Western culture: intuition. The scope of ecological connections, Carson asserts, can *only* be grasped by drawing on intuitive and imaginative modes that reveal the unity inherent in life's diversity.

An intuitive grasp of ecological relations can carry one beyond the constrictions of a narrow, ego-bound identity: "ecological thinking . . . requires a kind of vision across boundaries. The epidermis of the skin is ecologically like a pond surface . . . [not] a shell so much as a delicate interpenetration. It reveals the self as ennobled and extended . . . as part of the landscape and the ecosystem."[8] The expansive identity that characterizes ecological thought and practice can be likened to the unbounded consciousness that occurs in meditation. Writers may even have moments of mystical insight in which they see beyond conventional borders of awareness.

The impact of these revelations, though, depends on the credence that individuals give to them. Secular culture values efficient functioning over improbable grace: consequently, Scott Momaday notes, profound vision can be obscured by a utilitarian view that deems the world useful but not beautiful.[9] By resisting this conditioning, ecological converts come to see the world on its own terms and honor its revelations.

Their aesthetic mode of perception may prove therapeutic both for the individual and the collective. "We're given art to heal ourselves," Alice Walker believes, "and by extension to help other people heal themselves."[10] Art creates not just material objects but spiritual bonds, connections that can help restore the ecological whole. Creative expression can simultaneously transform inner and outer worlds (a theme developed in chapter 7).

Art can also foster community, linking people to one another and to the Earth. Ecological writers envision their words as weaving humans back into the ecological whole. When anticipating what she will write, poet Linda Hogan reflects: "I ask myself how best to let my words serve."[11] Her phrasing reveals a spiritual vision. She offers her words in service of something larger, a harmonious relationship with the Earth. Like other ecological writers, Hogan seeks to bear witness both to the rending of the ecological web and to the sacred integrity that endures amidst losses. Both forms of witness become a matter of moral, even religious, duty: to acknowledge the beauty inherent in the world is an act of reverence; to testify to ecological degradation is an act of atonement. Writers who bear witness to both these dimensions find that their work is religious in the original sense, binding together the whole of being. Their desire for a reconciliation with Earth leads them into resistance, challenging the societal forces and institutions that perpetuate environmental destruction.

Structures of Power

Ecological converts tend to distrust the technologies, corporations, and commercial media that serve—in their view—to reinforce a homogenized and vacuous consumer culture. They see these forces as inimical to human and ecological well-being. Edward Abbey, an anarchist by inclination and training, considered all institutions of dubitable value, but those that prevail in industrialized society he found especially abhorrent. Millions of citizens, he claimed, now feel "fear and detestation" at the "plastic-aluminum-electronic-computerized technocracy rapidly forming around us, constricting our lives to the dimensions of the machine, divorcing our bodies and souls from the earth."[12] Abbey considered these technological forces to be not just distasteful but inhumane, dividing humans from one another and the rest of nature. Because corporate capitalism, mechanization, and materialism sever the spiritual, moral, and physical bonds joining people to place, they can thwart efforts to live with ecological integrity. Those who challenge these pervasive forces tend to move from a state of passive resistance to one of radical criticism. "You can best serve civilization," they conclude, "by being against what usually passes for it."[13]

Converts work to obstruct the relentless corporate effort to standardize, upgrade, and streamline systems for maximum efficiency and minimal human or natural contact. They routinely challenge the assumptions used to justify technological "improvements": that material progress is an unmitigated good; that increased speed and efficiency are necessarily desirable; and that bigger is better. These unexamined assumptions, built on precarious moral foundations, can prove hazardous. What distinguishes human actions, Rachel Carson noted in a speech shortly before her death, "is that they have almost always been undertaken from the narrow viewpoint of short-range gain. . . . [In the technological age], if we know *how* to do something, we do it without pausing to inquire whether we *should*."[14] To make technological advances without ethical self-scrutiny, Carson concludes, is not only ill-advised but pathologically self-destructive.

Carson's *Silent Spring* vividly portrays the myopia that afflicted government and corporations in the technological boom following World War II. It reveals how the economic interests of chemical manufacturers drove governmental decision making, resulting in practices that jeopardized public health and ecological well-being. Following the book's release, Carson testified before Congress and appeared on national television programs. She did not relish the media spotlight but was gratified to have her concerns heard. Carson felt it was "in the deepest sense, a privilege as well as a duty to have the opportunity to speak out—to many thousands of people—

on something so important."[15] Her work of resistance sparked a widespread campaign that helped launch a new wave of environmental activism.

The impact of Carson's work can be attributed in large measure to her deep sense of moral conviction. The content of her argument was compelling, but it was her passionate concern for the Earth that often caught and held people's attention. Senator Abraham Ribicoff, who chaired the congressional subcommittee that heard Carson's testimony, recalled that her words were those of a "true believer."[16] In her writing and public appearances, Carson bore witness to what she saw as our moral duty to maintain nature's beauty and integrity.

Carson's success is notable in its singularity. Despite the emergence of a vocal environmental movement and the production of countless ecological books, no subsequent work has generated such a strong public response. Carson's lone victory points to the difficulty writers face in publishing protests against established corporate and governmental powers. Marketing pressures and fears of litigation often quell publishers' interest in iconoclastic ecological texts. Aldo Leopold searched for years in the 1940s to find a publisher willing to take *A Sand County Almanac,* a series of lucid essays that articulate the basis for a new ecological ethic. The manuscript was finally accepted mere days before his death and had to be edited and printed posthumously. A rejection letter that Leopold received illustrates the challenges facing writers whose work falls outside the mass-market concerns of mainstream publishing. Knopf editor Clinton Simpson wrote Leopold, in part: "I wonder if you would consider making a book purely of nature observations, with less emphasis on the ecological ideas which you have incorporated into your present manuscript? . . . these ecological themes are very difficult indeed to present successfully for the layman . . . [and] the idea that the various elements and forces of nature should be kept in balance would end by becoming monotonous."[17]

As Leopold and subsequent writers have learned, economic pressures often favor the production of entertaining books over those intended to provoke substantive reflection. A cultural penchant for escapism—evident in popular literature, advertising, and epidemic rates of addiction—can thwart efforts to disseminate challenging ideas. Widespread denial of outer ecological concerns diminishes the potential audience for environmental works—particularly those that focus on inner ecology, since mass media and mainstream publications tend to sidestep spiritual and ethical matters. Discussion of such topics is seen as particularly suspect if it challenges society's assumed right to exploit nature for maximal profit.

Grassroots Action

Recognizing the limits of verbal suasion, many ecological writers choose more direct means of resistance—ranging from radical, defensive efforts such as protest actions to protective and remedial approaches such as land conservation. Local grassroots action can strengthen bonds with the natural community and extend an ecological practice.

Edward Abbey came to perceive his community as a cause worthy of a lifetime's work. In the vast expanses of the Southwest, Abbey reported finding "something to fight for that will never desert me in my lifetime."[18] His passion for place led him to undertake monkey-wrenching, a deliberate effort to "oppose, resist and sabotage the contemporary drift toward a global technocratic police state."[19] Abbey depicted extreme cases of sabotage in fiction (such as a plot to blow up Glen Canyon Dam) but confined himself to lesser measures in practice. Biographers and friends report that Abbey removed billboards and sabotaged road-building machinery to slow the pace of highway construction. In his monkey-wrenching, Abbey condoned crippling constructed objects but opposed terrorism (acts of violence against living beings). His actions strike many readers as extreme, but he believed that the pace and magnitude of environmental destruction warranted a radical response. Abbey felt obligated not just to adopt new modes of living but to actively dismantle the old.

Others writers choose more moderate and gradual means of

change. Rachel Carson and Terry Tempest Williams, for example, have worked to conserve natural areas through legislative measures and outright acquisition. Carson described her efforts as a way to take "care of a spiritual security, by 'laying up treasures' in an earthly heaven."[20] The deliberate use of religious language denotes her conviction that land protection is holy work, a means of honoring the sanctity of Earth. Ecological resistance, for Carson, was as much a religious devotion as a political act.

Some writers practice the spiritual discipline of resistance through patient efforts to revive the health of depleted habitats. Wendell Berry and his family, for example, have spent decades restoring the ecological balance of their farm along the Kentucky River. Berry pursues the slow work of restoration using draft horses (rather than diesel-burning technology) and eschewing commercial pesticides and fertilizers.

Through land stewardship and conservation, writers become active participants in their home habitats. Attentive to seasonal changes, shifting species dynamics, and nuances in weather, they come to an understanding of place that surpasses technical knowledge. Their efforts to restore outer landscapes renew their inner connections to the whole, reinforcing a sense of reciprocity.

To express their kinship with other beings, some ecological writers advocate for animal welfare. Rachel Carson, a devoted amateur ornithologist and professional marine ecologist, saw her efforts to restrict pesticide use as vital to ensuring the health of wild and domesticated animals. She also voiced her concern for animals more directly—lobbying the Food and Drug Administration to free dogs used in laboratory research and writing Congress in support of reduced animal testing. Shortly before her death, Carson drafted the foreword to an exposé on factory farming called *Animal Machines*.

The kinship that poet Linda Hogan feels for animals finds expression in work caring for birds of prey injured by cars, shooting, trapping, or ensnarement. She describes her volunteer job in a wildlife rehabilitation center as an "apprenticeship" in which she is the "disciple of birds." Here again religious language reveals the spiritual quality of this bond. What the hawks, owls, and eagles require of their human caretakers, Hogan asserts, is that "we learn to be equal to them, to feel our way into an intelligence that is different from our own." She considers her rehabilitation work to be ecological restoration in the broadest sense, providing a tangible means of healing "the severed trust" between humans and the Earth.[21]

Political Testimony

Spiritual bonds with other creatures and with place can lead ecological writers into the political arena. Citizenship in the natural community obligates them to represent those who cannot participate directly in the civic process. Typically writers meet this responsibility through grassroots organizing, participation in nonprofit work, and legislative testimony. Alice Walker, Edward Abbey, Terry Tempest Williams, and numerous others have successfully followed Carson's lead in fusing political advocacy and creative writing.

Yet some writers hesitate to enter this charged sphere or even acknowledge that their writing has political implications. Despite the inspiration his work has given the American Indian movement, Scott Momaday denies being political: "that's not my disposition, somehow. I'm not a political person."[22] Momaday prefers to view his writing as moral: his focus rests on underlying values, not on the tactics of societal reform. This perspective may be particularly prevalent among Native American writers who tend to view politics, and the cycles of life, from a long-term perspective. Laguna Pueblo writer Leslie Marmon Silko asserts: "the most effective political statement I could make is in my art work. I believe in subversion rather than straight out confrontation. I believe in the sands of time."[23] This more oblique approach relies on individual reflection and communal reassessment rather than firsthand involvement in legislative initiatives. While less common among ecological writers than direct testimony, this path reveals an ambivalence shared by many of those who seek to fuse art and advocacy.

Writers who do engage in political activism rarely confine their public testimony to legislative hearing rooms. When politicians ignore their calls to action, converts may resort to acts of civil disobedience. They follow the dictates of conscience over the letter of the law. Through demonstrations and protests, they try to raise public consciousness and persuade those in power.

The precedent for such action, among ecological writers, was set by Henry Thoreau, who was jailed briefly for war tax resistance. Contemporary writers continue to risk imprisonment in protests against the military. Alice Walker has joined in numerous demonstrations and civil disobedience actions at military sites (protesting the export of arms to Central America), while Terry Tempest Williams has participated in direct actions at the Nevada nuclear testing site. Frustration with the legal system first sparked Williams's interest in civil disobedience: "to our court system it does not matter whether the United States government was irresponsible, whether it lied to its citizens, or even that citizens died from the fallout of nuclear testing. What matters is that our government is immune."[24] Williams concludes that a system capable of inflicting death on its own citizens must be changed.

Both Williams and Walker view their nonviolent protests as necessary to ensure the greater peace of the human and ecological community. Neither one distinguishes between peace and environmental actions: they see military destruction as one facet of an exploitative power structure that endangers all life. They declare their allegiance to Earth and act on its behalf, striving for an ideal of what Walker terms "conscious harmlessness."[25]

By stepping into the political fray, writers risk losing the contemplation and concentration needed for a creative life. Campaign strategizing and media outreach can drain them, while extensive travel deprives them of essential time with the people and places they love. One way to reach a middle path between civic responsibilities and creative needs, Terry Tempest Williams believes, is to serve a political tour of duty. In her vision of democracy, "each of us takes our turn [working on large-scale issues] and then we step back into community. . . . If we each take our turn, no one is beat up too much. No one gets too tired, too burned out. We realize that it's a rotation. And we can give each other strength and inspire one another."[26]

Williams followed this formula in her work for Utah wilderness preservation. On that issue, she reflects, her number came up. She poured energy into lobbying, grassroots organizing, and coediting the book *Testimony*, a chapbook on Utah wilderness lands distributed to every member of Congress. After President Clinton established the Grand Staircase-Escalante National Monument, Williams stepped back to work on local concerns. She recognizes that the issue of Utah wilderness preservation is far from resolved: it will resurface periodically as it has for generations. What is essential, she believes, is that "each generation takes its turn."[27]

Rachel Carson expressed similar sentiments during the political fervor following *Silent Spring*'s publication. Given Carson's media success, environmental activists anticipated a repeat performance. They asked Carson to undertake a sequel that would stimulate debate on other long-neglected environmental concerns. Carson's response was polite but firm: "One crusading book in a lifetime is enough."[28] Carson had devoted six years of her life to the research, writing, and public defense of *Silent Spring*. She rarely begrudged the demands imposed by the book and never seemed to consider abandoning the project despite a host of medical and personal crises. When she completed the manuscript, though, she sensed that her moral obligation was met. Carson wrote a friend expressing relief at having repaid her debt to the natural world: "Last night the thoughts of all the birds and other creatures and all the loveliness that is in nature came to me with such a surge of deep happiness, that now I had done what I could—I had been able to complete it—now it had its own life."[29]

In a world wracked by ecological ills, it can be hard for individuals to discern when their obligation to Earth is met. Carson is one of the few writers to make peace with what she could do. Even that relief may have been fleeting, more a consequence of exhaustion than conviction. Within months of concluding she had done what she could, Carson had thrown herself into public lectures, television appearances, and congressional testimony. Ecological writers face a relentless stream of issues that demand attention: they continually must balance their desire for ecological integrity with the exigencies of a society slow to change. Being a "counter-friction" to powerful societal forces can wear one down physically, emotionally, and spiritually, as many active writers attest. To sustain their commitment, they often strive to join resistance with reverence.

Resistance comprises measures taken against current practices and policies. It represents a reactive stance, often grounded in anger or fear. Reverence, in contrast, grows from awe, wonder, and profound humility. It is a sensual and spiritual affirmation of unity within seeming diversity and of integrity amidst apparent chaos. An ecological practice hinges on maintaining a precarious balance between these paradoxical forces. Writer E. B. White described this existential tension as being caught between a desire to save the world and a desire to savor it. The challenge, White and others conclude, is to hold the poles together—simultaneously savoring the world in revelatory moments and saving it through conscious acts of resistance.

For writers who dwell within this paradox, the art of savoring comes to inform the acts of saving. Their creative sensibilities and spiritual bonds to Earth continually shape their efforts at resistance. Conservation work becomes a form of spiritual devotion as well as political action. Carson, for example, termed her pesticide campaign a crusade, and Williams calls her wilderness advocacy a form of religious testimony. This fusion of the spiritual and political appears to strengthen their ecological practice. Devotional acts in the public sphere reinforce a sense of reciprocity and open the way to new visions for living in the world.

One Reader's Resistance

The call to act on behalf of Earth has always come to me in stereo—prompted by both outer and inner ecology. A passion for place propels my turn toward Earth, while a stern conscience steers me from destructive environmental habits. I can't fully explain the source of this strong moral compass, unless it traces back to ancestral roots in puritanical New England. I do know that I began to feel its pull early in life. A letter written to a cousin when I was eight or nine begins: "Have you herd [sic] that they want to Build an oil Refinery in the Bay? Please write to Every Body and ask them not to." Even at that tender age, I sensed the need to take pen in hand—trying to defend a place I loved.

That impulse grew stronger with time, and by high school I was working on political campaigns and lobbying for alternative energy and against nuclear power and weaponry. For several years, I focused on issues that were national or international in scope, seeing those as the most urgent and significant.

Then, sometime during college, I discovered works on "voluntary simplicity" that prompted me to rethink the scale on which I was working. I began to see that nearly all of my daily decisions involving diet, transportation, material goods, and recreation affected the broader natural community (including other humans around the world). Wanting to reduce the impact of my "ecological footprint," I gave up eating factory-farmed meat and began to purchase food in bulk, shop at thrift stores and consignment shops, and run errands by bicycle.

This idealistic focus on living ecologically intensified, rather than diminished, in the years following college. Working for a range of organizations, I was struck by how often environmental work becomes a profession like any other, pursued with a certain detachment from one's personal life. Even dedicated and well-intentioned environmental professionals end up commuting absurd distances, flying extensively to meetings, routinely using disposable products, and making a host of other lifestyle choices that counter the goals they espouse.

I couldn't escape all these contradictions within my own life, but I became increasingly conscious of the gaps that remained between my ecological values and daily actions. To help myself and others live with greater integrity, I began teaching community education classes in "Shopping for a Better Environment." The best thing for the Earth, of course, would be to not shop at all, but living requires consuming some resources. The challenge is to consume moderately and mindfully, conscious of our ecological wake.

This domestic approach to resistance pales beside more dramatic and large-scale protests, yet I remain convinced of its importance. Ecology, as its Greek roots confirm, begins in our households. Political action becomes indistinguishable from daily living when we support local organic growers, advocate for and use safe bikeways, and minimize consumption of material goods. If our ecological practice starts at home and extends outward, then eventually the mundane domestic decisions will begin to transform our communities.

My efforts at more direct community action have been political by default. Like Scott Momaday, I don't define myself as a political person: my need for privacy runs counter to that public role. Yet I step into the political sphere when circumstances and conscience dictate action. A life removed from politics seems like a luxury we can no longer afford.

Even small efforts to serve as a "counter-friction" to destructive cultural forces may buy time for a broader and deeper societal transformation. How that collective turn to Earth will come about remains to be seen. I still hold a child's faith, though, that taking pen in hand, mobilizing friends, and writing to "Every Body" may bring a change for the better.

7

Ritual

To create is to involve oneself as fully, as consciously,
as possible in the creation, to be immersed in the world.
—Wendell Berry in Merrill, *The Forgotten Language*

In turning to Earth, ecological converts routinely engage in devotional acts that celebrate and strengthen their ties with the sacred whole. Rituals provide a way to embody their values and beliefs, expressing their spiritual passion for the natural world. Each ritual constitutes a turn within a turn, a gesture that represents and reinforces a more encompassing life transformation. By performing these sacred acts, ecological converts join more fully and consciously in re-creating the world.

Among all the elements of ecological conversion, ritual is the hardest to characterize. It is at once a deeply personal and universal impulse to honor the ineffable dimensions of being. Even ecological writers are often reticent in the realm of ritual, unwilling to diminish sacred experience through inadequate description. There is no formal taboo against documenting their rituals (as there is in many primal cultures), yet converts appear wary of offending the divine by divulging too much.

The ritual practices that support a turn to Earth typically fall outside the bounds of institutional religion, yet they are profoundly religious in the oldest sense—binding individuals into the greater whole. Ritual helps converts honor the essential unity of inner and outer ecology, transmuting the fundamental relation of physical interdependence into a spiritual and moral communion. It satiates converts' deep hunger for belonging, allowing them "not only to express the inexpressible, but to enter into it."[1] In this respect, the rituals involved in a turn to Earth are akin to more conventional religious rites: they provide a symbolic fusion of the individual and the collective.

Rituals can accelerate the process of turning by reinforcing and integrating other elements of conversion. They can awaken remembrances, recalling the unbounded identity of youth when one lived fully in place and time. They can steady one in the deep trench of reflection, reaffirming a cyclical view of life that places struggles and setbacks within a larger context. They can spark revelation by leading one to see the world anew. Meaningful rituals can affirm one's essential kinship with other beings. They can even become a means of resistance, countering the solitary, passive, and technological forms of entertainment that dominate Western culture. By reviving communal forms of creative expression such as ritual, storytelling, and ceremony, converts challenge the entrenched individualism that exacerbates ecological problems. The sacred rituals in which they engage reinforce a sense of community that encompasses other species and the land.

Ecological converts typically adapt ritual forms from different faith traditions (particularly Earth-based ones) and draw on their own imaginations to create simple but meaningful acts and practices that honor their bonds to the Earth. Some of these rites are spontaneous; others become routine, evolving over time as conversions deepen. Even everyday acts of devotion can take on "sacramental value" through a "systematic practice" of ritual.[2]

Devotional Writing

The reflective practice of writing appears to help converts experience and record the dynamic interplay between inner and outer ecology. "When we are drawn into the element of language," Scott Momaday observes, "we are as intensely alive as we can be; we create and are created."[3] Language attunes us to the ongoing creation, enabling us to experience the mystery that inheres in the world.

Terry Tempest Williams describes writing as a ritualized way of "walking into unknown territory." She treats the practice of writing as sacred, lighting a candle and placing a bowl of water and a treasured rock on her writing space. These objects symbolize for her the spirit that moves through one, the source behind the words. The work of writing does not involve willful artistry so much as watchful patience and trust. She likens the creative process to birthing, noting that one may have to carry a story for months, even years, before it comes to term. That gestation is part of the spiritual practice of writing, she observes: "you hold those stories until it's their time . . . ; it's about mindfulness."[4]

Viewing writing as an exercise in mindfulness can help extend consciousness beyond the confines of individual identity so that writing comes to reflect the creative energy animating the whole: "I think you touch into the mythstream that is always there . . . [a] part of the world," notes writer Paula Gunn Allen. "Instead of asserting 'I wrote that piece,' a writer will acknowledge, 'I listened.'"[5] This perspective is common among ecological writers: rather than seeing their work as a personal achievement, they consider it one manifestation of a universal creativity evident throughout the natural world. No one writer, therefore, can claim a monopoly on truth: "I believe that the truth about any subject only comes when all sides of the story are put together, and all their different meanings make one new one," Alice Walker asserts. "Each writer writes the missing parts to the other writer's story."[6] We depend on each other in the creative search for meaning just as we do in an ecological context. In both cases, Walker suggests, diversity strengthens the integrity of the whole.

The practice of writing can become a means of affirming spiritual belonging within that whole: "It is in nature writing—perhaps almost as much as in wilderness itself—that I learn to recognize the shape and force of my own desire to be at home on the earth," writer SueEllen Campbell observes.[7] The reflective act of sculpting experience into language, she suggests, helps to situate us within a broader community—joining us both to the rich soil of lived experience and the ineffable realm of spirit.

Writing can foster a deep appreciation of the sacred even among those distant from conventional religions. Edward Abbey, a self-described "Earthiest" who grounded his faith in the "apodictic rock" beneath his feet, still saw his craft as a devotional practice. The land constituted Abbey's religion and writing his primary means of honoring the sacred. "Writing is a form of piety or worship," he observed. "I try to write prose psalms that praise the divine."[8] A devotional practice of writing brings converts closer to an ongoing experience of the sacred in daily life.

Approaching writing as a spiritual discipline requires quieting the mind and body through a process of deliberate centering. Scott Russell Sanders begins each day writing in this meditative manner "in order to come more fully awake."[9] His expression echoes Thoreau's famous injunction: "We must learn to reawaken and to keep ourselves awake."[10] Awakening represents spiritual enlightenment, an intensity of being that humans rarely if ever realize. The ideal of complete awakening may prove elusive, but converts strive toward that vision through the art of attentiveness and the discipline of writing.

Sharing Stories

Because words are a powerful force in their own lives, ecological writers believe that stories can help other people "feel the ache and tug of the organic web."[11] Converts' accounts of turning become a form of seedstock harvested from the Earth and passed on to others who might cultivate and exchange stories. Ecological writers hope that the growth of this collective garden may return narrative to a central place in Western culture (which prefers the seeming precision of scientific materialism to the archetypal power and subtle wisdom revealed in stories). Through the ritual exchange of stories, converts simultaneously foster both cultural and ecological restoration.

The transformative power of words is greatest, they readily admit, in spoken language. Cultures rich in oral storytelling experience language not as a cognitive construct but as a "sensuous, bodily activity born of carnal reciprocity and participation."[12] Words simultaneously derive from and reinforce that embodied exchange: "In the oral tradition," Scott Momaday notes, "words are sacred; they are intrinsically powerful and beautiful."[13] The storyteller need not impart these qualities to a narrative: the story itself becomes a window into the grace that inheres in the world.

To experience the power of oral storytelling and incorporate it into their work, ecological writers may immerse themselves in indigenous cultures. Terry Tempest Williams, for example, spent a year living among the Navajo—an experience that helped her recognize how personal stories can affirm shared ground and build community (whether defined by family, region, spirituality, or politics). "Storytelling awakens us to that which is real," she writes: "It is the most pure form of communication because it transcends the individual. . . . Those things that are most personal are most general, and are, in turn, most trusted. Stories bind. They are connective tissues."[14] The ritual exchange of stories, she finds, can reinforce a sense of reciprocity within and beyond our own species.

Narratives can also prompt reflection and awaken the conscience. Apache elder Benson Lewis describes how this potent moral prod can evoke a more conscious pattern of living: "Stories go to work on you like arrows. Stories make you live right. Stories make you replace yourself."[15] In mainstream Western culture, where few people still rely on narrative to gain their moral bearings, this power is lost. Those without guiding stories are often adrift, unable to find ways to live right.

Ecological converts strive to fill this cultural void by crafting and sharing stories that affirm our collective bonds with the natural world, sustaining the health of both people and land. "To restore any place," writer Gary Paul Nabhan observes, "we must also begin to re-story it, to make it the lesson of our legends, festivals and seasonal rites."[16] Nabhan's work as an ethnobotanist—preserving native plant species and the indigenous cultures built around them—gives him insight into how narrative and ritual arts help to re-place people within the greater whole. Many communities with whom Nabhan works lost crucial environmental knowledge when mass media and formal schooling became the dominant means of informational exchange. People stopped sharing stories and legends about how and why certain plants grew, diminishing both their practical knowledge and their spiritual affinity for place. When story no longer served as a ritualized means of remembrance, people readily become estranged from their home ground. The path to ecological restoration, Nabhan now believes, depends on sustaining stories that reinforce communal ties to native habitat.

Narrative provides an essential channel of communication and communion between people and land: "through the stories," writer Paula Gunn Allen observes, "the gap between isolate human being and lonely landscape is closed."[17] In her view—common to many ecological writers—the land needs to be celebrated and honored through story and ritual. This perspective echoes the Aboriginal conviction that "an unsung land is a dead land."[18] Land dies when deprived of a harmonious relationship with its inhabitants. Restoring that bond requires a devoted practice of place-based ritual and story. Terry Tempest Williams, for example, sees her participation in direct actions at the Nevada nuclear testing site as a ritualized means of restoring a dead land wracked by atomic detonations. By entering the site in festive costumes, dancing, and singing, Williams and her colleagues hope to generate a new story—and hence a new future—for the land and those beings who live on or in it.

When land is not celebrated through communal stories and rituals, it can be vulnerable. Scott Russell Sanders recalls what befell the unsung geography of his youth. The rural region of Ohio where he lived was populated by small-scale farmers, many of whom were devoted to the land. When the federal government proposed constructing a dam that would flood their fertile valley, no one organized resistance. Families were bought out and relocated, watching helplessly as their land was drowned. Sanders speculates that the absence of shared stories contributed to this collective displacement: "Our attachments to the land were all private. We had no shared lore, no literature, no art to root us there, to give us courage to help us stand our ground."[19]

Having learned from that loss, Sanders now works to build a communal lore that can help sustain the land and those who live by it. He has spent years traveling the back roads of Indiana, gathering stories from long-time residents and sharing them through essays so that others will have an art to root them in place. His efforts to re-story home terrain have deepened Sanders's ecological practice and sense of moral responsibility. "I am bound to earth," he writes, "by a web of stories." The bond is covenantal, made for life: Sanders describes himself as married to the land "by narrative as well as nature."[20] Many ecological writers express similar convictions, affirming the power of story to reinforce and celebrate their intimate ties to place.

Offerings

The ongoing exchange between people and place can come to resemble a potlatch, a lavish gift-giving ritual among Pacific Northwest Indians that fosters impulsive generosity.[21] Ecological converts bask in the Earth's fecundity and, in return, acknowledge its bounty and beauty through story and ritual offerings. Their ceremonial rites become gestures of thanks, gifts given in honor of gifts received.

This exchange requires wholehearted participation. Terry Tempest Williams reflects on the role these ceremonial rites play in sustaining the balance between the temporal and sacred: "I've always had this overriding sense that there is something much larger circulating through our world. And we're part of it and it moves through us. There are certain obligations and rituals suggested that are very serious [and] that must be maintained. . . . I have felt the weight of that responsibility."[22] Honoring the sacred forces at work in the world, she holds, is not an option but an obligation.

The range of forms that these offerings can take is almost limitless—from momentary prayers to more deliberate and extended ceremonies. Some expressions may even be spontaneous, arising in the course of everyday activities. Even simple and impromptu rituals can serve as acts of spiritual devotion. Edward Abbey, for example, describes an evening in canyon country when he set up camp, built a cedar fire, and began playing flute. His music was a song for place, he reflected: he was "doing only what is proper and necessary."[23] By undertaking these small gestures with reverential care, Abbey celebrated his deep sense of reciprocity and belonging.

Alice Walker finds that ceremonial gestures can reawaken her to the spirit that inheres in the elemental world. "It is my habit as a born-again pagan to lie on the earth in worship," she writes. "In this, I imagine I am like my pagan African and Native American ancestors, who were sustained by their conscious inseparability from Nature."[24] By physically prostrating herself on the ground, Walker affirms the depth of her spiritual attachment to the natural world.

Whereas conventional religious rites may be weighty and elaborately programmed, the sacred acts of ecological converts tend to grow from a playful and imaginative engagement with place. In her story "The Stone Spiral," Terry Tempest Williams illustrates how a simple game to pass time evolves into a lengthy ritual that reflects the dynamic confluence of landscape and imagination. A couple assembles rocks in a spiral tracing the color spectrum from black center stone to white outer stone. Each stone is awarded a domain of creation, with tales told of the creatures it rules. The couple brings water to quench the stones' thirst and inscribes the sand by each one with a family member's name. Every dimension of this ceremony binds the participants more deeply to place until the stones literally become family. Williams's account demonstrates how ritual ceremonies can root people within the larger natural community, reviving a familial intimacy with other species and the elemental world.

Offerings that foster this felt conviction of reciprocity can reinforce a turn to Earth.

Many ecological writers strive for a life in which these sacred acts are a seamless part of their daily routine rather than a periodic interlude. Although this ideal is hard to realize in modern Western culture, members of some primal societies do achieve it: they spend only 30 percent of their time "working," anthropologists have observed. The remainder is devoted to rituals, dance, and ceremony.[25] Even this distinction may be misleading, so closely allied are their work and ceremony.

Ecological writers seek to experience a similar fusion by treating writing as a spiritual offering. Alice Walker describes her work as "a prayer to and about the world."[26] Prayer, she believes, serves as "the active affirmation in the physical world of our inseparableness from the divine; and everything, especially the physical world, is divine."[27] Weighing her work by this spiritual measure helps Walker extend the role of sacred ceremony in her life.

By reaffirming physical and spiritual connections with the living world through ritual, Walker and other converts cultivate greater faith in the potential for ecological healing and change. They come to believe with poet Linda Hogan that "the earth cranes its neck to hear our prayers."[28] This deep trust in the possibility for spiritual and ecological renewal becomes the axis of their turning: "Faith is the centerpiece of a connected life," Terry Tempest Williams observes. "It allows us to live by the grace of invisible strands."[29] The faith she describes is not a naïve conviction that all will turn out for the best or that divine intervention will repair the devastation humans have wrought on the Earth. The faith that sustains ecological converts—in all aspects and phases of their turning—is a trust in humans' capacity to hear the Earth's prayers and respond.

The convert's path of deepening devotion is akin to the creative process, which is slow and arduous but rich in unexpected rewards. We "might grow into faith much as one writes a poem," reflects writer Kathleen Norris. "It takes time, patience, discipline, a listening heart. There is precious little certainty, and often great struggling, but also joy in the discoveries."[30] By engaging in the creative acts of writing, storytelling, and ceremony, ecological converts learn how to live with a "listening heart," fostering the wakeful receptivity and compassion needed in a turn to Earth.

One Reader's Ritual

Knowing that the process of turning often moves in a spiral, I should not have been surprised to find reflections on ritual leading back to the remembrance of youth. Like most children, I came to know the world through spontaneous ritual.

Place-based rituals dominate my collage of childhood memories. The ones that remain most vivid are those that brought me into contact with the elemental world. There were our daily "swims" on the island each June where we flailed through icy waters, too shocked by the cold to move in any coordinated fashion. Emerging from the bay, lungs gasping, we would throw ourselves down on sun-warmed towels and feel tingling sensation return to our fingers and toes. There were nighttime walks at my grandparents' home, a 1700s farmhouse nestled into a hillside along a narrow country lane. Late in the evening, we would walk up that road beneath a canopy of leaves so dense that it completely obscured the night sky. Going through that ink-black tunnel of trees taught me early to trust my instincts in situations where I could not see. When we reached the crest of the hill, we would turn from the paved surface onto a dirt road that led between cornfields. There the world opened wide before us—a broad arc of constellations above a patchwork of gently rolling fields and woods. The stars, undimmed by any city lights, seemed almost as close as the lights that emanated from the few visible houses. Conversation dwindled into reverent silence as we breathed in the palpable peace of that scene.

Many of the rituals I engage in now hearken back to those days. I am an avid walker, having learned early what new worlds open up when one slows down to sauntering speed. I still find a greater peace feeling my way by starlight and moonlight than I can find in the bustle and glare of daytime activity. And I continue to immerse my-self in the elements—swimming in icy waters, basking on sun-warmed rocks, and venturing outdoors to experience the wild force of storms.

What is new since childhood is the impulse to offer thanks: I now feel impelled to acknowledge the grace and suffering of others and to honor the miraculous that abides within the everyday world. Not to *notice* the color purple when you walk by it in a field (as Alice Walker reflects) is an act of acedia that diminishes our own lives and the Spirit that inheres in the whole.

To remind myself to partake fully and thankfully in the blessings of being, I rely on the Sanskrit phrase *Jai Bagwan*. It means, I am told, "I bow to the light within you"—a phrase that echoes the Quaker conviction that an inner light illumines each being. This ges-ture of spiritual recognition helps reaffirm my reciprocity with other beings, within and beyond my own species. It provides a way to acknowledge loss, offered as a form of prayer to those who suffer due to violence, disease, and tragedy. It serves as a heartfelt apology—to the animals we callously call "road kills," to the birds that feed on chemically treated lawns and fields, to the wild creatures we deprive of homes, and to the countless other victims of our heedlessly de-structive ways. It also acts as a grace, honoring the beauty and com-passion that thrive amidst so much waste and destruction.

This small offering, made to other individuals and the world at large, helps me to live with a "listening heart." It renews my empa-thy with fellow beings and strengthens my resolve to work on behalf of Earth.

Epilogue

As my work on this project drew to a close, I gave birth to a son. Bennet's new life gives greater meaning and poignancy to the questions I have about our ecological future. There is a bittersweet edge as I watch him explore his surroundings with infinite curiosity. Instead of meeting a world worthy of his pure trust, he faces a beleaguered environment. The warming sun that should be a welcome presence has become a threat. Even the breast milk that symbolizes motherly love bears a load of accumulated contaminants.

I want for my son what should be each child's birthright: clean air and water; wholesome, untainted food; and strong roots in a community intimately bound to the natural world. Seeking what is best for him renews my commitment to ecological restoration. The vision of Native Americans who weigh the effects of their actions over seven generations still eludes me, yet even stretching my sight to embrace the span of Bennet's life recasts my responsibility as a parent and a citizen of Earth. It is no longer enough to seek what is best for my child: I need to work for the health of the whole—knowing that ultimately the two goals are indistinguishable.

The stories of ecological converts inspire and guide me in this process by provoking critical questions. How can I help Bennet be at home in the natural world, living with wakeful senses and a compassionate heart? How can I live with greater ecological integrity myself, knowing how much he may learn from his parents' example?

These questions propel my turn to Earth. Taking to heart the advice of poet Rainer Maria Rilke, I strive to live the questions now—trusting that eventually I may live my way into the answers.

Beginning Anew

Bennet has much to teach me about living the questions. He faces life as a bright-eyed beginner, humble and joyful before the mystery of being. His hungry mind and alert senses trace the contours of language and land as he absorbs indelible impressions of place. Outdoors Bennet typically settles into a quiet, alert mode—serene as a heron poised waiting for fish. Perhaps every young child has this capacity for ready communion with his surroundings. (If so, then each turn to Earth is indeed a "re-turning," learning anew how to be truly still and attentive.)

Rediscovering the world through Bennet's wide-open senses reminds me of the joy inherent in an intimate bond with Earth. He is a connoisseur of being, relishing the sensory smorgasbord that each place and moment offer. (Even as I write this, he is meditating on a blade of grass—his chubby fingers wrapped around its slender stalk as he systematically examines it sense by sense.) Bennet's insatiable curiosity tests the façade of knowing I have built up through years of formal schooling: his questions run circles around my answers, revealing how little of life I truly understand.

Watching him explore, I cannot help but wonder how different the world might be if—in the process of "growing up"—we did not lose this wholehearted capacity to engage with the natural world and to honor spirit in all its guises. If we could retain or regain this openness, we might enjoy a greater capacity for revelation and reciprocity and have less tolerance for heedless destruction.

To sustain a wakefulness to the natural world, we must resist the accelerating treadmill of modern life and accommodate ourselves more to the measured pace of childhood. Rachel Carson advocated in *The Sense of Wonder* for adults to join with young people in explorations outdoors—delighting in the daybreak chorus of birds, the elemental force of storms, and the shimmering mystery of moon-drenched vistas. We need to conserve open space not only in our landscapes but in the terrain of our personal lives—allowing time for reflection and ritual. Our souls crave stillness, unadorned beauty, and a deep sense of belonging. The accounts of ecological converts affirm the inestimable worth of giving children ample time to nourish their souls in the natural world: few choices we make as parents may shape their lives as strongly.

Tending to Place

A vital lesson I have gained from reading natural autobiographies is that a turn to Earth is propelled not by fear or guilt, but by love—a deep and enduring attachment to place. The directive to dwell more fully in place recurs so frequently in ecological writing that it can seem like a truism, an innocuous—even nostalgic—refrain. Yet following this call in a restless, rootless society may be one of the most radical acts we can take.

In our work to revive links with the land, we may learn from those who know the meaning of home. Several years ago I interviewed a teacher on a remote island after two of her students won prizes in the national *River of Words* writing contest. She attributed their success to the self-understanding that comes from a strong connection to one's native ground. All her students know what matters to them in life, she said, because they have the gift of being limited in what they can do: they are removed from much of pop culture and immersed in the island's natural cycles.

That gift may be one of most enduring ones that we can share with our children. To provide for Bennet a stable home base and some critical distance from aimless materialism, my husband, Ed, and I have chosen a life of deliberate limits. We have put down roots in a small community and declined opportunities that would require long commutes, extensive travel, or frequent moves.

Here we will try to live in keeping with place, learning alongside Bennet as he grows. He will guide us in sensory awareness, and we will strive to help him understand how the land sustains him and how he can nurture it. The terrain of home will be a primary teacher during his formative years, helping to cultivate a vivid sense of life's unfathomable mysteries. It strikes me as ironic and sad that nearly all the transformative moments ecological converts describe occur outside traditional educational settings. The institutions that could foster a turn to Earth—such as schools, camps, and mass media— too rarely do, promoting conformity and certitude rather than an abiding sense of wonder.

To help Bennet sustain that enduring awe, Ed and I will share our enthusiasm for the natural world, conveying a sense for how each being fits within the whole. We will try to foster Bennet's innate sympathy for other species while teaching appropriate boundaries. All too often in our culture wild creatures are seen as existing solely for human amusement, a "Disneyfication" of nature that undermines any hope of genuine reciprocity between species. We will try instead to forge a relationship with other beings that joins compassion with respect for their sovereignty.

Given our strong environmental concerns, it would be easy as parents to push Bennet into early activism—reasoning that the sooner he learns about complex crises, the sooner he can contribute to meaningful change. That path, while tempting, no longer seems like the soundest way to foster a conversion. Well-intentioned efforts to teach young children about global problems like rainforest destruction and climate change can backfire, leaving children feeling helpless and hopeless rather than connected and committed. The deep empathy and responsible action we seek to encourage only comes through a slow process of bonding with place.

A commitment to "save" the Earth grows from time spent savoring its beauty and goodness. Like every young child, Bennet is an expert in savoring and will help us learn anew the subtleties of this art. The joy we share being outdoors will inform our family's efforts to live with ecological integrity and resist the destructive pressures of a culture that is materially driven and spiritually adrift.

Living Deliberately

The stories of ecological converts and my own experience of turning have convinced me that dwelling at the margins of mainstream culture holds untold benefits, despite its negative connotations. Reflecting on the variation between my own inner compass and the course set by the larger society prompts me to seek a more encompassing view of the "good life," one not defined by power or possessions. It helps me follow Thoreau's counsel to "live deliberately" and simply, appreciating the holy moments and attending to the larger whole.

Many of the measures that Ed and I take to minimize our ecological wake are not pursued in a spirit of resistance: they derive as much from thrift and personal preference as they do from principle. Yet the response that even these mundane choices evoke continually reminds me that they are profoundly countercultural.

One morning recently as Ed hung out Bennet's cloth diapers, a neighbor called over to offer the use of her clothes dryer—a humorous dig at our "backward" ways. Ed tried to explain that we prefer to hang clothes outdoors: it gives us a chance to enjoy the morning air and it leaves our clothes smelling wonderful. Similarly, we would rather burn a few calories pushing our reel lawn mower than breathe exhaust fumes and listen to the irritating whine of a two-stroke engine. We love to move around town under our own power, walking or biking, free from parking headaches and traffic backups. We are not depriving ourselves of coveted "conveniences" or seeking to score in some environmental virtuosity contest: the choices that are easier on Earth and more economical happen to be more appealing.

Growing up with the creative tension between our household norms and those of the larger culture may prompt Bennet to question many societal practices (and some familial ones!). He undoubtedly will reach an age where he resists our acts of resistance and wants to indulge more in the excesses of the broader culture. I'm sure he'll struggle at times with the practices that define our family life (having no television, eating natural foods, and striving for minimal and mindful consumption of energy and goods). Ultimately, though, I hope he will find that a life less weighted by material gadgetry and distractions yields greater meaning and fulfillment. Through moments of reflection and revelation in his own turn to

Earth, Bennet may come to value more enduring sources of contentment: true companionship; communion with place; creative arts and rituals; and the moment-to-moment gratitude in being that constitutes lived prayer.

Notes

Acknowledgments

1. Conway, *True North*, 34.

Introduction

1. Rockefeller, *John Dewey*, 114.
2. Griffin, *Turning*, 10.
3. Tallmadge, "John Muir," 65.
4. Jensen, *Listening to the Land*, 129.
5. Abbey, *Journey Home*, 65.
6. Buber, *I and Thou*, 58.
7. Boff, *Ecology and Liberation*, 168.
8. Conn, *Conversion Perspectives*, 55.
9. Thoreau, *Walden*, 186.
10. Slovic, *Seeking Awareness*, 18.
11. McClintock, *Nature's Kindred Spirits*, 20.
12. Kroeber, *Nature of Culture*, 320.
13. Williams, interview by author.
14. Albanese, *Nature Religion in America*, 155.
15. Brockelman, *Cosmology and Creation*, 119.
16. Rambo, *Understanding Religious Conversion*, 17.
17. Loder, *Transforming Moment*, 3–4.

18. Brockelman, *Cosmology and Creation*, 119–39.
19. Merton, "Letter," n.p.
20. Loder, *Transforming Moment*, 19.
21. James, *Varieties of Religious Experience*, 244.
22. Williams, *Desert Quartet*, 44.

1. Bedrock

1. Williams, interview by author.
2. Ibid.
3. Abbey, *Desert Solitaire*, 268.
4. Sanders, *Staying Put*, 175.
5. Libby, "Writing Our Refuge," 2.
6. Williams, *Refuge*, 135.
7. Williams, interview by author.
8. Ibid.
9. Frost, *Poetry of Robert Frost*, 377.
10. Williams, interview by author.
11. Carson, *Sense of Wonder*, 45.
12. Williams, interview by author.
13. Williams, "Bedrock Democracy," 107.
14. Williams, "Hearing Stories," 20.
15. Williams, interview by author.
16. Williams, *Refuge*, 4.
17. Williams, interview by author.
18. Williams, *Refuge*, 178.

19. Williams, *Unspoken Hunger*, 127.
20. Williams, *Refuge*, 285–86.
21. Ibid., 121.
22. Ibid., 5.
23. Eliot, *Collected Poems*, 186.
24. Abbey, *Voice Crying in the Wilderness*, 12.
25. Williams, *Refuge*, 285.
26. Ibid., 246.
27. Williams, interview by author.
28. Williams, *Refuge*, 24.
29. Ibid., 286.
30. Jensen, *Listening to the Land*, 311.
31. Williams, *Refuge*, 231.
32. Jensen, *Listening to the Land*, 312.
33. Ibid., 314.
34. Williams, *Refuge*, 240.
35. Jensen, *Listening to the Land*, 313.
36. Williams, interview by author.
37. Williams, *Unspoken Hunger*, 64.
38. Ibid., 86.
39. Williams, interview by author.
40. Ibid.
41. Williams, *Red*, 84.
42. Williams, *Refuge*, 286.
43. Williams, interview by author.
44. Bush, "Terry Tempest Williams's *Refuge*," 157–58.
45. Williams, *Desert Quartet*, 46.
46. Williams, interview by author.
47. Williams and Trimble, eds., *Testimony*, 7.
48. Williams, interview by author.
49. Williams, *Red*, 19.
50. Williams, *Unspoken Hunger*, 133.
51. Ibid., 78.
52. Williams, interview by author.
53. Merton, "Hagia Sophia," 506.
54. Williams, *Pieces of White Shell*, 69.
55. Williams, interview by author.
56. Williams, *Refuge*, 235.
57. Williams, *Timpanogos*, n.p.

2. Remembrance

1. Lopez, "Conference Excerpt," 3.
2. Momaday, *Man Made of Words*, 39.
3. Sanders, *Staying Put*, 12.
4. Momaday, *Man Made of Words*, 77.
5. Cobb, *Ecology of Imagination in Childhood*, 88.
6. Williams, interview by author.
7. Williams, *Art of the Wild*.
8. Abbey, *Down the River*, 111.
9. Walker, *Anything We Love*, 129.
10. Cousineau, ed., *Hero's Journey*, 8.
11. Bruchac, ed., *Songs from This Earth*, 92.
12. Chawla, *First Country of Places*, 43.
13. Woodard, *Ancestral Voice*, 44.
14. Hurston, *Dust Tracks on a Road*, 41.
15. Leopold, *Sand County Almanac*, 251.
16. Sobel et al., "Pocketful of Stones," 28.
17. Barbato, *Heart of the Land*, 282.

18. Abbey, *Journey Home*, 224.
19. Williams, *Refuge*, 33.
20. Sanders, *Country of Language*, 9.
21. Hinchman, "Naturalist's Journal," 63.
22. Sanders, *Writing from the Center*, 171.
23. Sanders, *Paradise of Bombs*, 7.
24. Abbey, *Journey Home*, 225.
25. Walker, *Same River Twice*, 24.
26. Sanders, *Secrets of the Universe*, 230.
27. Sanders, *Staying Put*, 186.
28. Momaday, *Way to Rainy Mountain*, 8.
29. Carson, *Sense of Wonder*, 45, 52.
30. Brooks, *House of Life*, 242.
31. Ibid.
32. Williams, *Refuge*, 119.
33. Brooks, *House of Life*, 110.
34. Williams, interview by author.
35. Snyder, *Practice of the Wild*, 61.
36. Sanders, *Writing from the Center*, 170.
37. Williams, "Bedrock Democracy," 105.
38. Nabhan and Trimble, *Geography of Childhood*, 30.
39. Orr, *Earth in Mind*, 161.
40. Cather, "Neighbor Rosicky," 88.

3. Reflection

1. Williams, interview by author.
2. Griffin, *Turning*, 136.
3. Loder, *Transforming Moment*, 37.
4. Glendinning, My *Name Is Chellis*, 109.
5. Carson, *Always, Rachel*, 248–49.
6. Berry, *Long-Legged House*, 25.
7. Abbey, *Confessions of a Barbarian*, 309.
8. Sanders, *Writing from the Center*, 61.
9. Carson, *Always, Rachel*, 227.
10. Abbey, *Abbey's Road*, 195.
11. Hardy, *Spiritual Nature of Man*, 81.
12. Sanders, *Paradise of Bombs*, 65.
13. Thoreau, *Walden*, 80.
14. Albanese, *Nature Religion in America*, 99.
15. Williams, *Refuge*, 29.
16. Beston, *Outermost House*, 25.
17. Abbey, *Journey Home*, 208.
18. Williams, *Refuge*, 242–43.
19. Ibid., 244.
20. Ehrlich, *Solace of Open Spaces*, x.
21. Carson, *Always, Rachel*, 332.
22. Brooks, *House of Life*, 228.
23. Ibid., 327.
24. Brockelman, *Cosmology and Creation*, 120.
25. Walker, *Same River Twice*, 32.
26. Ibid., 32.
27. Macy, *World As Lover*, 22.
28. Sanders, *Staying Put*, 121.
29. Sanders, *Writing from the Center*, 173.
30. Gates and Appiah, *Alice Walker*, 327.
31. Kelsey, *Companions on the Inner Way*, 17.

32. Bishop, *Epitaph for a Desert Anarchist*, 37.
33. Allen, *Sacred Hoop*, 9.
34. Balassi, Crawford, and Eysturoy, *This Is about Vision*, 7.
35. Williams, interview by author.
36. Gates and Appiah, eds., *Alice Walker*, 328.
37. Ibid., 330.
38. Schweitzer, *Light within Us*, 25–26.

4. Revelation

1. Levertov, *Light up the Cave*, 288.
2. Lyon, *This Incomperable Land*, 19.
3. Abbey, *Abbey's Road*, 195.
4. Aton, "Interview with Barry Lopez," 16.
5. Hanh, *Being Peace*, 38.
6. Lindbergh, *Gift from the Sea*, 109.
7. Underhill, *Mysticism*, 331.
8. Sanders, *Writing from the Center*, 7.
9. Ibid., 8.
10. Loder, *Transforming Moment*, 17, 24.
11. Carson, *Always, Rachel*, 204.
12. Kelsey, *Companions on the Inner Way*, 12.
13. Abbey, *Journey Home*, 65.
14. Leopold, *Sand County Almanac*, 138.
15. Ibid., 240.
16. Bama, "Unseen Mountain," 50–51.
17. Ibid., 52.
18. Abbey, *Beyond the Wall*, 52–53.
19. Abbey, *Journey Home*, xiii.
20. Carson, *Always, Rachel*, 59.
21. Woodard, *Ancestral Voice*, 13.
22. Nabhan and Trimble, *Geography of Childhood*, 36.
23. Conn, *Conversion Perspectives*, 144.
24. Allen, *Sacred Hoop*, 147.
25. Momaday, *Man Made of Words*, 114.
26. Arrien, "Spirit," 152.
27. Sanders, *Country of Language*, 36.
28. Bishop, *Epitaph for a Desert Anarchist*, 17.
29. Balassi, Crawford, and Eysturoy, *This Is about Vision*, 55.
30. Nelson, *Island Within*, 52.
31. Rockefeller, "Faith and Community," 160.
32. Wolfe, *John of the Mountains*, 137–38.
33. Walker, *Anything We Love*, 3.
34. Highwater, *Primal Mind*, 76.
35. Oliver, *New and Selected Poems*, 94.
36. Slovic, "Nature Writing and Environmental Psychology," 351.
37. Fox, *American Conservation Movement*, 367.
38. Brooks, *House of Life*, 2.
39. Bruchac, ed., *Survival This Way*, 186.
40. Abbey, *Beyond the Wall*, 45.
41. Loder, *Transforming Moment*, 119.

5. Reciprocity

1. White, *Talking on the Water*, 170.
2. Carson, *Edge of the Sea*, viii.
3. Eiseley, *All the Strange Hours*, 153.
4. Carson, *Edge of the Sea*, 5.
5. Sanders, *Writing from the Center*, 123.
6. Slovic, "Nature Writing and Environmental Psychology," 352.
7. Walker, *Living by the Word*, 143.
8. Sanders, "Honoring the Given World," 29.
9. Nelson, *Island Within*, 27.
10. Snyder, *Practice of the Wild*, 184.
11. Schweitzer, *Out of My Life and Thought*, 186.
12. Abbey, *Abbey's Road*, 135.
13. Noddings, *Caring*, 18.
14. Bruchac, *Songs from This Earth*, 23.
15. Berry, *Long-Legged House*, 143.
16. Capps, *Seeing with a Native Eye*, 80.
17. Sanders, "Landscape and Imagination," 66.
18. Moore, "Ecology: Sacred Homemaking," 138–39.
19. Nelson, *Island Within*, 185.
20. Cahill, ed., *Writing Women's Lives*, 95.
21. Williams, *Refuge*, 288.
22. Momaday, *Man Made of Words*, 114.
23. Tallmadge, *Meeting the Tree of Life*, 186.
24. Harrison, *Making the Connections*, 13.
25. Balassi, Crawford, and Eysturoy, *This Is about Vision*, 62.
26. Carson, "Of Man and the Stream of Time," 8.
27. Gablik, "A Few Beautifully Made Things," 41.

6. Resistance

1. Thoreau, "Resistance to Civil Government," 63.
2. Roszak, Gomes, and Kanner, eds., *Ecopsychology*, 91.
3. Buell, *Environmental Imagination*, 138.
4. Brooks, *House of Life*, 13.
5. Ibid., 228.
6. Belenky, *Women's Ways of Knowing*, 101.
7. Carson, *Edge of the Sea*, vii–viii.
8. Bowers, *Education, Cultural Myths*, 204.
9. Woodard, *Ancestral Voice*, 69.
10. Gates and Appiah, *Alice Walker*, 322.
11. Balassi, Crawford, and Eysturoy, *This Is about Vision*, 154.
12. Abbey, *Abbey's Road*, 126.
13. Berry, *Continuous Harmony*, 42.
14. Carson, "Of Man and the Stream of Time," 10.
15. Carson, *Always, Rachel*, 259.
16. Lear, *Rachel Carson*, 454.

17. Callicott, *Companion to "A Sand County Almanac,"* 99.
18. Abbey, *Confessions of a Barbarian,* 8.
19. Abbey, *One Life at a Time,* 177.
20. Carson, *Always, Rachel,* 214.
21. Hogan, *Dwellings,* 148, 150, 153.
22. Balassi, Crawford, and Eysturoy, *This Is about Vision,* 63.
23. Coltelli , *Winged Words,* 147–48.
24. Williams, *Refuge,* 285.
25. Walker, *Anything We Love,* 42.
26. Williams, interview by author.
27. Ibid.
28. Lear, *Rachel Carson,* 452.
29. Brooks, *House of Life,* 272.

7. Ritual

1. Martin, "Joining of Human, Earth, and Spirit," 54.
2. Tallmadge, *Meeting the Tree of Life,* 164.
3. Momaday, *Man Made of Words,* 169.
4. Williams, interview by author.
5. Balassi, Crawford, and Eysturoy, *This Is about Vision,* 105.
6. Walker, *In Search of Our Mothers' Gardens,* 49.
7. Campbell, "Land and Language of Desire," 136.
8. Abbey, *Abbey's Road,* 195.
9. Sanders, *Writing from the Center,* 177.
10. Thoreau, *Walden,* 79.
11. Sanders, *Secrets of the Universe,* 226.
12. Abram, *Spell of the Sensuous,* 82.
13. Momaday, *Man Made of Words,* 104.
14. Williams, *Pieces of White Shell,* 134–35.
15. Nabhan and Trimble, *Geography of Childhood,* 21.
16. Nabhan, *Desert Legends,* 193.
17. Allen, *Sacred Hoop,* 120.
18. Chatwin, *Songlines,* 52.
19. Sanders, *Writing from the Center,* 5.
20. Sanders, *Staying Put,* 150, 167.
21. Snyder, *Practice of the Wild,* 19.
22. Williams, interview by author.
23. Abbey, *Abbey's Road,* 195.
24. Walker, *Same River Twice,* 25.
25. White, *Talking on the Water,* 122.
26. Walker, *Same River Twice,* 38.
27. Walker, *Living by the Word,* 192.
28. Bruchac, Hogan, and McDaniel, eds. *Stories We Hold Secret,* 282–83.
29. Williams, *Refuge,* 198.
30. Norris, *Cloister,* 61.

Works Cited

Abbey, Edward. *Abbey's Road*. New York: Dutton, 1979.

———. *Beyond the Wall: Essays from the Outside*. New York: Holt, 1984.

———. *Confessions of a Barbarian: Selections of the Journals of Edward Abbey, 1951–1989*. Edited by David Peterson. Boston: Little, 1994.

———. *Desert Solitaire: A Season in the Wilderness*. New York: Dutton, 1977.

———. *Down the River*. New York: Dutton, 1982.

———. *The Journey Home: Some Words in Defense of the American West*. New York: Dutton, 1977.

———. *One Life at a Time, Please*. New York: Holt, 1988.

———. *A Voice Crying in the Wilderness: Notes from a Secret Journal*. New York: St. Martin's, 1989.

Abram, David. *The Spell of the Sensuous: Perception and Language in a More-than-Human World*. New York: Pantheon, 1996.

Albanese, Catherine L. *Nature Religion in America: From the Algonkian Indians to the New Age*. Chicago: University of Chicago Press, 1990.

Allen, Paula Gunn. *The Sacred Hoop: Recovering the Feminine in American Indian Traditions*. Boston: Beacon, 1986.

Arrien, Angeles. "Spirit in Action: In Service of the Earth and Humanity." In *The Soul of Nature: Celebrating the Spirit of Earth*, edited by Michael Tobias and Georgianne Cowan. New York: Plume: 1996.

Aton, Jim. "An Interview with Barry Lopez." *Western American Literature* 21, no. 1 (1986): 3–17.

Balassi, William, John F. Crawford, and Annie O. Eysturoy. *This Is about Vision: Interviews with Southwestern Writers*. Albuquerque: University of New Mexico Press, 1990.

Bama, Lynne. "The Unseen Mountain." In *The Earth at Our Doorstep: Contemporary Writers Celebrate the Landscapes of Home*, edited by Annie Stine. San Francisco: Sierra, 1996.

Barbato, Joseph, and Lisa Weinerman, eds. *Heart of the Land: Essays on Last Great Places*. New York: Pantheon, 1994.

Belenky, Mary Field, Blythe Cinchy, Nancy Goldberger, and Jill Tarule. *Women's Ways of Knowing: The Development of Self, Voice, and Mind.* New York: Basic, 1986.

Berry, Thomas. *The Dream of the Earth.* San Francisco: Sierra, 1988.

Berry, Wendell. *A Continuous Harmony: Essays Cultural and Agricultural.* New York: Harcourt, 1970.

———. *The Long-Legged House.* New York: Harcourt, 1969.

√Beston, Henry. *The Outermost House: A Year of Life on the Great Beach of Cape Cod.* New York: Viking, 1956.

Bishop, James, Jr. *Epitaph for a Desert Anarchist: The Life and Legacy of Edward Abbey.* New York: Atheneum, 1994.

Boff, Leonardo. *Ecology and Liberation: A New Paradigm.* Maryknoll: Orbis, 1995.

Booth, Annie L., and Harvey M. Jacobs. "Ties that Bind: Native American Beliefs as Foundation for Environmental Consciousness." *Environmental Ethics* 12 (1990): 27–43.

Bowers, C. A. *Education, Cultural Myths, and the Ecological Crisis: Toward Deep Changes.* Albany: State University of New York Press, 1993.

Brockelman, Paul. *Cosmology and Creation: The Spiritual Significance of Contemporary Cosmology.* New York: Oxford, 1999.

Brooks, Paul. *The House of Life: Rachel Carson at Work.* Boston: Houghton, 1972.

Bruchac, Carol, Linda Hogan, and Judith McDaniel, eds. *The Stories We Hold Secret: Tales of Women's Spiritual Development.* Greenfield Center: Greenfield Review Press, 1986.

Bruchac, Joseph, ed. *Songs from This Earth on Turtle's Back: Contemporary American Indian Poetry.* Greenfield Center: Greenfield Review Press, 1983.

———. *Survival This Way: Interviews with American Indian Poets.* Tuscon: Sun Tracks and University of Arizona Press, 1987.

Buber, Martin. *I and Thou.* Edited by Walter Kaufmann. New York: Scribner's, 1970.

Buell, Lawrence. *The Environmental Imagination: Thoreau, Nature Writing, and the Formation of Environmental Culture.* Cambridge: Harvard University Press, 1995.

Bush, Laura L. "Terry Tempest Williams's *Refuge*: Sentimentality and Separation." *Dialogue: A Journal of Mormon Thought* 28, no. 3 (fall 1995) 147–60.

Cahill, Susan, ed. *Writing Women's Lives: An Anthology of Autobiographi-*

cal Narratives by Twentieth-Century American Women Writers. New York: Harper, 1994.

Callicott, J. Baird, ed. *Companion to "A Sand County Almanac."* Madison: University of Wisconsin Press, 1987.

Campbell, SueEllen. "The Land and Language of Desire." In *The Ecocriticism Reader: Landmarks in Literary Ecology,* edited by Cheryll Glotfelty and Harold Fromm. Athens: University of Georgia Press, 1996.

Capps, Walter Holden, ed. *Seeing with a Native Eye: Essays on Native American Religion.* New York: Harper, 1976.

Carson, Rachel. *Always, Rachel: The Letters of Rachel Carson and Dorothy Freeman, 1952–1964.* Edited by Martha Freeman. Boston: Beacon, 1995.

———. *The Edge of the Sea.* Boston: Houghton, 1955.

———. "Of Man and the Stream of Time." *Scripps College Bulletin* 36, no. 4 (1962): 5–11. (Courtesy of Scripps College Archives.)

———. *The Sense of Wonder.* New York: Harper, 1965.

———. *Silent Spring.* Boston: Houghton, 1962.

Cather, Willa. "Neighbor Rosicky." In *Five Stories.* New York: Vintage, 1956.

Chatwin, Bruce. *The Songlines.* New York: Penguin, 1988.

Chawla, Louise. *In the First Country of Places: Nature, Poetry, and Childhood Memory.* Albany: State University of New York Press, 1994.

Cobb, Edith. *The Ecology of Imagination in Childhood.* Dallas: Spring, 1977.

Coltelli, Laura. *Winged Words: American Indian Writers Speak.* Lincoln: University of Nebraska Press, 1990.

Conn, Walter, ed. *Conversion Perspectives on Personal and Social Transformation.* New York: Alba House, 1978.

Conway, Jill Ker. *True North: A Memoir.* New York: Knopf, 1994.

Cousineau, Phil, ed. *The Hero's Journey: Joseph Campbell on His Life and Work.* San Francisco: Harper, 1990.

Dorsey, Peter A. *Sacred Estrangement: The Rhetoric of Conversion in Modern American Autobiography.* University Park: Pennsylvania State University Press, 1993.

Ehrlich, Gretel. *The Solace of Open Spaces.* New York: Penguin, 1985.

Eiseley, Loren. *All the Strange Hours.* New York: Scribner's, 1975.

Eliot, T. S. *Collected Poems: 1909–1962.* New York: Harcourt, 1963.

Emerson, Ralph Waldo. *Selected Essays.* New York: Penguin, 1982.

Fowles, John. *The Tree.* Photographs by Frank Horvat. Boston: Little, 1979.

Fox, Stephen R. *The American Conservation Movement: John Muir and His Legacy.* Madison: University of Wisconsin Press, 1986.

Frost, Robert. *The Poetry of Robert Frost.* Edited by Edward Connery Lathem. New York: Holt, 1979.

Gablik, Suzi. "A Few Beautifully Made Things." *Common Boundary* (March-April 1995): 41–46.

Gates, Henry Louis, Jr., and K. A. Appiah, eds. *Alice Walker: Critical Perspectives Past and Present.* New York: Amistad, 1993.

Glasgow, Ellen. *The Woman Within.* New York: Harcourt, 1954.

Glendinning, Chellis. *My Name is Chellis and I'm in Recovery from Western Civilization.* Boston: Shambhala, 1994.

Griffin, Emilie. *Turning: Reflections on the Experience of Conversion.* Garden City: Doubleday, 1980.

Hanh, Thich Nhat. *Being Peace.* Edited by Arnold Kotler. Berkeley: Parallax, 1987.

Hanh, Thich Nhat, et al. *For the Future to Be Possible.* Berkeley: Parallax, 1993.

Hardy, Alister. *The Spiritual Nature of Man: A Study of Contemporary Religious Experience.* Oxford: Clarendon, 1979.

Harrison, Beverly Wildung. *Making the Connections: Essays in Feminist Social Ethics.* Boston: Beacon, 1985.

Highwater, Jamake. *The Primal Mind: Vision and Reality in Indian America.* New York: Penguin, 1987.

Hinchman, Hannah. "A Naturalist's Journal as a Path to Place." Interview. In *Stonecrop: A Natural History Book Catalog.* Denver: River Lee, winter 1997. Commercial book catalog.

Hogan, Linda. *Dwellings: A Spiritual History of the Living World.* New York: Simon, 1995.

Hull, Fritz, ed. *Earth and Spirit: The Spiritual Dimension of the Environmental Crisis.* New York: Continuum, 1993.

Hurston, Zora Neale. *Dust Tracks on a Road.* New York: Harper, 1996.

James, Williams. *The Varieties of Religious Experience: A Study in Human Nature.* New York: Random, 1936.

Jensen, Derrick. *Listening to the Land: Conversations about Nature, Culture, and Eros.* San Francisco: Sierra, 1995.

Kellert, Stephen R., and E. O. Wilson, eds. *The Biophilia Hypothesis.* Washington, D.C.: Island, 1993.

Kelsey, Morton. *Companions on the Inner Way: The Art of Spiritual Guidance.* New York: Crossroad, 1985.

Kroeber, A. L. *The Nature of Culture.* Chicago: University of Chicago Press, 1952.

Lear, Linda. *Rachel Carson: Witness for Nature.* New York: Holt, 1997.

✓Leopold, Aldo. *A Sand County Almanac.* New York: Ballantine, 1966.

Levertov, Denise. *Light up the Cave.* New York: New Directions, 1981.

Libby, Brooke. "Writing Our Refuge: Autobiographizing a Self in Nature." Paper presented at the second biennial conference of the Association for the Study of Literature and the Environment, University of Montana, Missoula, 19 July 1997.

✓Lindbergh, Anne Morrow. *Gift from the Sea.* New York: Random, 1975.

Loder, James. *The Transforming Moment.* 2d ed. Colorado Springs: Helmers and Howard, 1989.

Lopez, Barry. "Conference Excerpt: Barry Lopez." *ASLE News* 9, no. 2 (1997): 3.

Lyon, Thomas, ed. *This Incomperable [sic] Land: A Book of American Nature Writing.* Boston: Houghton, 1989.

Macy, Joanna. *World as Lover, World as Self.* Berkeley: Parallax, 1991.

Martin, Daniel. "The Joining of Human, Earth, and Spirit." In *Earth and Spirit: The Spiritual Dimensions of the Environmental Crisis,* edited by Fritz Hull. New York: Continuum, 1993.

McClintock, James I. *Nature's Kindred Spirits: Aldo Leopold, Joseph Wood Krutch, Edward Abbey, Annie Dillard, and Gary Snyder.* Madison: University of Wisconsin Press, 1994.

McFague, Sallie. *The Body of God: An Ecological Theology.* Minneapolis: Fortress, 1993.

Meeker, Joseph W. *The Comedy of Survival: Studies in Literary Ecology.* New York: Scribner's, 1972.

Merrill, Christopher. *The Forgotten Language: Contemporary Poets and Nature.* Salt Lake City: Peregrine Smith, 1991.

Merton, Thomas. "Hagia Sophia." In *A Thomas Merton Reader,* edited by Thomas P. McDonnell. New York: Doubleday, 1974.

———. Letter. *Information Catholiques Internationale* (April 1973): back cover.

Momaday, N. Scott. *The Man Made of Words: Essays, Stories, Passages.* New York: St. Martin's, 1997.

———. *The Way to Rainy Mountain.* Albuquerque: University of New Mexico Press, 1969.

Moore, Thomas. "Ecology: Sacred Homemaking." In *The Soul of Nature: Celebrating the Spirit of Earth,* edited by Michael Tobias and Georgianne Cowan. New York: Plume, 1996.

Nabhan, Gary Paul. *Desert Legends: Re-storying the Sonoran Borderlands.* New York: Henry Holt. 1995.

Nabhan, Gary Paul, and Stephen Trimble. *The Geography of Childhood: Why Children Need Wild Places.* Boston: Beacon, 1994.

Nelson, Richard. *The Island Within.* New York: Random, 1991.

Noddings, Nel. *Caring: A Feminine Approach to Ethics and Moral Education.* Berkeley: University of California Press, 1984.

Norris, Kathleen. *The Cloister Wall.* New York: Riverhead, 1996.

Oliver, Mary. *New and Selected Poems.* Boston: Beacon, 1992.

Orr, David W. *Earth in Mind: On Education, Environment, and the Human Prospect.* Washington, D.C.: Island, 1994.

Rambo, Lewis. *Understanding Religious Conversion.* New Haven: Yale University Press, 1993.

Rich, Adrienne. *The Fact of a Doorframe: Poems Selected and New 1950–1984.* New York: Norton, 1994.

Rockefeller, Steven C. "Faith and Community in an Ecological Age." In *Spirit and Nature: Why the Environment Is a Religious Issue,* edited by Steven C. Rockefeller and John C. Elder. Boston: Beacon, 1992.

———. *John Dewey: Religious Faith and Democratic Humanism.* New York: Columbia University Press, 1991.

Roszak, Theodore, Mary E. Gomes, and Allen D. Kanner, eds. *Ecopsychology: Restoring the Earth, Healing the Mind.* San Francisco: Sierra, 1995.

Sanders, Scott Russell. *The Country of Language.* Minneapolis: Milkweed, 1999.

———. *The Force of Spirit.* Boston: Beacon, 2000.

———. "Honoring the Given World." Interview. In *Stonecrop: A Natural History Book Catalog,* 27–31. Denver: River Lee, summer 1997. Commercial book catalog.

———. *Hunting for Hope: A Father's Journey.* Boston: Beacon, 1998.

———. "Landscape and Imagination." *North American Review* 274, no. 3 (1989): 63–66.

———. *The Paradise of Bombs.* Athens: University of Georgia Press, 1987.

———. *Secrets of the Universe: Scenes from the Journey Home.* Boston: Beacon, 1991.

———. *Staying Put: Making a Home in a Restless World.* Boston: Beacon, 1993.

———. *Writing from the Center.* Bloomington: Indiana University Press, 1995.

Schweitzer, Albert. *The Light within Us.* New York: Philosophical Library, 1959.

———. *Out of My Life and Thought: An Autobiography.* New York: Holt, 1933.

Slovic, Scott. "Nature Writing and Environmental Psychology." In *The Ecocriticism Reader: Landmarks in Literary Ecology,* edited by Cheryll Glotfelty and Harold Fromm. Athens: University of Georgia Press, 1996.

———. *Seeking Awareness in American Nature Writing.* Salt Lake City: University of Utah Press, 1992.

Snyder, Gary. *The Practice of the Wild.* New York: Farrar, 1990.

Sobel, David, et al. "A Pocketful of Stones: Memories of Childhood." *Orion* 12, no. 2 (spring 1993): 28–37.

Strong, Douglas H. *Dreamers and Defenders: American Conservationists.* Lincoln: University of Nebraska Press, 1988.

Tallmadge, John. "John Muir and the Poetics of Natural Conversion." *North Dakota Quarterly* 59, no. 2 (spring 1991): 62–79.

———. *Meeting the Tree of Life: A Teacher's Path.* Salt Lake City: University of Utah Press, 1997.

Thoreau, Henry David. *The Journal of Henry D. Thoreau.* Vol. 9. Edited by Bradford Torrey and Francis H. Allen. Boston: Houghton Mifflin, 1906.

———. "Resistance to Civil Government." In *Reform Papers,* edited by Wendell Glick. Princeton: Princeton University Press, 1973.

———. *Walden or Life in the Woods.* Garden City: Anchor, 1973.

Underhill, Evelyn. *Mysticism.* New York: Penguin, 1974.

Walker, Alice. *Anything We Love Can Be Saved: A Writer's Activism.* New York: Random, 1997.

———. *The Color Purple.* New York: Washington Square Press, 1982.

———. *In Search of Our Mothers' Gardens: Womanist Prose.* New York: Harcourt, 1983.

———. *Living by the Word: Selected Writings 1973–1987.* San Diego: Harcourt, 1988.

———. *The Same River Twice: Honoring the Difficult.* New York: Scribner, 1996.

White, Jonathan. *Talking on the Water: Conversations about Nature and Creativity.* San Francisco: Sierra, 1994.

Williams, Terry Tempest. "A Bedrock Democracy." *Audubon* (May-June) 1996: 120.

———. Featured writer. *Art of the Wild.* Bayland Productions, 1996. Videocassette.

———. *Coyote's Canyon.* Salt Lake City: Peregrine Smith, 1989.

———. *Desert Quartet: An Erotic Landscape.* New York: Pantheon, 1995.

———. "Hearing Stories, Finding Family, Returning Home." *High Country News*, 10 June 1996, p. 20.

———. Interviews by author. Salt Lake City, Utah, 9–10 July 1996; and 8 November 1997.

———. *Pieces of White Shell: A Journey to Navajoland*. Albuquerque: University of New Mexico Press, 1984.

———. *Red: Passion and Patience in the Desert*. New York: Pantheon, 2001.

———. *Refuge: An Unnatural History of Family and Place*. New York: Random, 1991.

———. *Timpanogos: A Prayer for Mountain Grace*. Comp. Kurt Bestor. Utah Symphony Chorus. Maurice Abravanel Hall, Salt Lake City. Performed 10 July 1996.

———. *An Unspoken Hunger: Stories from the Field*. New York: Random, 1994.

Williams, Terry Tempest, and Stephen Trimble, eds. *Testimony: Writers of the West Speak on Behalf of Utah Wilderness*. Minneapolis: Milkweed, 1996.

Wolfe, Linnie Marsh. *John of the Mountains*. Madison: University of Wisconsin Press, 1979.

Woodard, Charles L. *Ancestral Voice: Conversations with N. Scott Momaday*. Lincoln: University of Nebraska Press, 1989.

Acknowledgments

Researching the contours of ecological conversion led me into the academic outback, a wild and creative setting free from the boundaries denoting traditional disciplines. On this journey, I received a wealth of guidance and support from faculty members and administrators, friends, and family.

My advisor, Paul Brockelman, and committee members—Melody Graulich, Barbara Houston, Sarah Way Sherman, and Tom Sullivan—were true guides. They provided essential direction while sharing in the exploratory spirit of this reconnaissance. From the outset, they recognized that this project was more than an academic exercise for me. Historian Jill Ker Conway recalls being told by her graduate advisor: "One's research should always involve some element of therapy. . . . It only counts if it's really close to the bone."[1] My research does strike close to the bone, and my committee honored and supported that dimension of the work. In their capacity to join intellectual rigor and compassionate concern (for their students and the world at large), they are exemplary teachers.

The University of New Hampshire, where I undertook much of this study, demonstrated vision and commitment in supporting my unconventional research. The Natural Resources Doctoral Program (under John Aber's capable leadership) provided an academic niche for this interdisciplinary work. The Farrington Fund, within the Department of Natural Resources, generously helped cover my conference travel expenses on several occasions. In my time at UNH, I was fortunate to share the companionship of three wonderful fellow scholars: Cathy Clipson, Penelope Morrow, and Mary Westfall.

I am indebted to John Elder, of Middlebury College, who has been a source of inspiration and moral support. His writings and grassroots work have raised the profile of ecological writing and highlighted the spiritual need for a conversion to Earth. The Association for Study of Literature and the Environment and the Orion Society have also been tremendous resources.

Staff at the University of Virginia Press helped shepherd this work through a long revision process. I greatly appreciate the insight and patience of editors Cathie Brettschneider, Ellen Satrom, and Susan Brady.

I will never know what prompted Terry Tempest Williams, amidst overflowing life demands, to agree to being interviewed for this work, but I am immensely grateful that we were able to connect. Her generous heart and gracious spirit inform this work: she inspires by example.

Heartfelt thanks go to Elizabeth Farnsworth, Cindy Krum, and Alix Hopkins, cherished friends and kindred spirits. Dorrie, my canine companion for sixteen wonderful years, taught me how much joy resides in the present moment.

Through the long and unconventional course of my educational journey, my parents—Peter and Polly Schauffler—have consistently supported my independent path. I am grateful beyond measure for their abiding love. My grandparents Marnie and Ben Schauffler left a legacy of kinship that continues to nourish our family and a place that will sustain each generation to come.

My husband, Ed Geis, has taught me that the turn to Earth can be a shared journey: I can imagine no better traveling companion. Our beloved son, Bennet, gives us great joy and renewed reason to take good care of the Earth.

Lastly, I give thanks to this rugged, island-rich coast. Here my spirit is moored.

Index

"ECOLOGICAL LINKAGES" HURST/READER   45

ACEDIA - SPIRITUAL TORPOR + APATHY

SANDERS' HAWK/FATHER. 77, 78 -
[WILLIAMS' OWL / MOTHER

G. NABHAN ? (DESERT bk)